THE NE
ULTRA VVEIRD

THE NEW NEW ULTRA WEIRD

ADAM GLASIER & RICHARD SCHUMACHER | *EDITORS*

"It was a dark and stormy night…"
—Edward Bulwer-Lytton

THE SYNTHESIS

| INCEPTION: THE BIRTH OF A PARADIGM | III
HAROLD LAUDER

CATALYZERS

| VERSE | 1
AMANDA MCKITTRICK ROS

| MOON PEOPLE | 3
DALE M. COURTNEY

| THE EYE OF ARGON | 23
JIM THEIS

| CONFRONTATION | 55
SARRA ELISEN

| SILK AND STEEL, AN EXCERPT | 61
RON MILLER

VOMITORIUM

| BEING BORN | 71
BERTRAND RUSSELL

| DOGGY DOO | 73
DAISY STARCHILD

| FALLEN ANGEL | 79
STRETCH ARMSTRONG

| Black and White read |
LISA NAPERTMENTE   87

| Disenchanted Enchantment | 89
QUENTIN NELSON

| The Frankfurter | 99
WILLIAM BEAN

| Tar God | 107
MARTIN BERNARD

| Cleanup | 117
CLARA TEE

| Spit and Swallow | 121
FRANCIS IGUANA

| Where the Wild Things Aren't | 137
JASON J. JONES

| The Aliens Who Ruined Everything | 149
BARRY BAXTER

Confabulation

The New New Ultra Weird: A Heated
Debate   169

Recommended Reading   181

Acknowledgements

We'd like to thank everyone for their contributions to this book. First to our publishers, whom we have never met or spoken to, and to our proofreaders, who do not exist. Thanks also goes to Gary Busey, our artistic guru and the well of our wisdom, and the Dread Lord Cthulhu for the supply of coffee and donuts. Our greatest grattitude goes to the writers of these stories, who will probably never publish anything ever again.

THE NEW NEW ULTRA WEIRD

THE INCEPTION
THE BIRTH OF A PARADIGM

Genesis

WHILE THE "NEW NEW ULTRA WEIRD" HAS only recently been accepted by certain fringe factions of the literary community as an authentic genre, it has its origins in a spirit of storytelling older than the written word itself. Like the literary equivalent of Atlas, it raises two great arms—one reaching for the deep and mystical origin of the human imagination, the other reaching ahead to explore the vast unknown future of all art, civilization, and thought itself. Unlike any genre before it, stories in the New New Ultra Weird are not simply the result of creative labor, but tap into the original process of writing. Rather than goggle at a fine-tuned product, this genre explores the struggle of searching and discovering, and in the midst of this struggle attempt to answer humanity's deepest questions: Who am I? What is my purpose? Should I order fries with that quarter-pounder? Until now, every book written over centuries and millennia has come closer and closer to achieving the one story that will complete all other stories. That ultimate story, the master narrative, the monomyth of Joseph Campbell, begins in the pages of the book you bear in your hands.

The earliest of writers whose work could justifiably be the first literature to foment this genre scholars agree was the Irish writer Amanda McKittrick Ros. In 1897, her first novel *Irene Iddesleigh* was published with her own expenses, but she remained obscure throughout her life. The world was simply not ready for the new style of her prose. Of her novels and poems, even Aldous Huxely wrote that:

"We see... the result of the discovery of art by an unsophisticated mind and of its first conscious attempt to produce the artistic. It is remarkable how late in the history of every literature simplicity is invented."

Throughout her lifetime, Ros was a famously mocked writer—the Inklings, a group of writers and scholars, whose notable members included J. R. R. Tolkien and C. S. Lewis, made a party game out of her poems and novels by reading her work aloud while straining not to laugh. Despite the world's rejection of her work, Ros continued to persevere writing stories until the very end.

Much like the early writers of science fiction and pulp, this new genre was heavily stereotyped simply as a venue for publishing instead of a scholarly mode of writing. Before the advent of self-publishing, writers of the new genre were never published at all—their style of prose was rejected simply as "bad" writing. If they earned fame, it was from sheer mockery, and not acceptance of the many diverse and divergent forms of writing. Publishing companies, the gatekeepers of the literary world, have kept most writers of the New New Ultra Weird in the darkness from the public, because the genre disregards and completely reinvents the standards which traditional presses deem a "good" piece of literature.

Despite major opposition against the authority of publishers, the New New Ultra Weird has surfaced in other less conventional ways besides the usual venues of publication. Clearly Jim Theis's *The Eye of Argon* has influenced the high fantasy genre as much as Tolkein or Pierce Anthony, despite never being formally published. Theis's manuscript caught the attention of the editor. It was rejected, but the editor was so taken by its ravishing prose and ambitious style that he passed it to another editor, who showed it to friends, and the story subsequently reached the public by its sheer popularity. It's another fabulous example of a writer who in his moment was mocked, but in scholarly retrospect has been recognized as a landmark contributor to a new wave of science fiction writers commonly called the New New Ultra Weird.

Self-publishing, which has not been widely available until recent, has acted as the watershed for this new wave, bringing writers of the New New Ultra Weird style to the front stage. In 2010, the Xlibris Company published Dale M. Courtney's epic space opera *Moon People*. After the book's publication, along with its two sequels, there was a heated debate among hundreds of Amazon reviewers. Courtney's book received five stars, and it immediately caught the attention of editors, writers, and agents of all kinds. There was praise, outrage, and profound confusion. A new mode of thought, a new way to tell stories, was born. One critic, so altered by the avante garde perspectives of genre and form in Courtney's work, responded with the following statement:

I realized the linguistic flexibility that comes from releasing character speech from its quotation marks. There is a certain joy that comes with exercising the freedom to end a sentence on any punctuation, even a comma. Question marks needn't be for interrogative statements! Must we bind every interjection to an exclamation point? Henceforth we shall be free to transpose homophones with the confidence that the reader will still get the point. Even chapters needn't be logical containers for portions of the story; why can't we start a new chapter in the middle of a conversation with two characters? Even the rules of spelling and capitalization serve only to bestow an unnecessary magniloquence when plain conversational writing will do. After reading this book, I scoff even at the concept of 'correct' word order.

Courtney's literary success has led to a growing fringe community of writers who challenge the conventions of snobby Oxford scholars and educators of English. That Amazon review thread, which has influenced the world of fantasy, science fiction, and horror at breathtaking speed, has changed the literary market forever. You can see it for yourself in the later sections of this anthology.

What is most distinct about this genre is that its concept did not spawn merely in the mind of one writer, mind you, but because of its origins in the collective human conscious we see it has been seemingly invented by several minds in several periods of history. At its rawest interpretation, the brainchild of what has evolved into the greatest literary movement of the human age was also seeded in the mind of yet another science fiction writer, Carter Scholz, before he published his debut short story "The Nine Billion Names of God" along with "The Last Question" and made literary history. In a letter to an editor who had yet to see this author's brilliance, at a time when the struggling writer was still aspiring for publication, Scholz explained the essential truth that drives every writer of the New New Ultra Weird:

You may find a story in a tree, but never a tree in a story, only the constellation of letters tree, and the crushed remains of one in the paper. Why tell stories if all the stories that ever could be are told constantly in the wind and the rain? That is the real last question: do we need fiction? Do we need science? I think we do not, most of us (Kelly 98)[1].

Depressing as Scholz's conclusion may have been, it was this newfound perspective of utter nihilism that gave rise to the greatest stories of our time. The complete surrender to the pointlessness of the product of art and the meaninglessness of signs manufactured solely by human evolution has influenced a new wave of writers.

The style and issues associated with the New New Ultra Weird have become a quintessentially important influence on cinema. Any film that stars Pauly Shore is, of course, directly inspired by the works of this genre. *Killer Clowns From Outerspace* was the first movie to deal with the marginalization of circus performers in the United States[2]. However, the New New Ultra Weird did not solidify as a genre in film until the release of *The Room* in 2003. *Bad Milo*

---

1. Kelly, James P., and John Kessel, eds. *The Secret History of Science Fiction*. San Francisco, CA: Tachyon Publications, 2009. Print.
2. I think we all remember the banana cream pie incident of 1946.

THE NEW NEW ULTRA WEIRD

shifted focus from sweeping societal concerns to the personal—it was a lesson of self-control and coming to terms with one's id, as well as a deconstruction of father-son relationships and the limits of proctology. The New New Ultra Weird was also introduced into film documentaries, when the History Channel aired *Ancient Aliens*, which by its uncanny ability to present such vast numbers of facts and yet prove virtually nothing about anything it at all demonstrates Scholz's philosophy on writing: the rule of futilism. We would characterize the New New Ultra Weird not only as profoundly intuitive about the nature of human beings, but also about major concerns in a post-post-modern society.

Definition

Okay. So nobody actually KNOWS what the New New Ultra Weird is. Most people have never even heard of it. We don't even know what it is, and hell, we're the editors. It probably doesn't even exist yet. It might already be dead. But we didn't let that stop us from making an anthology about it.

Simply put, this genre defies convention. Since the ancient days when man chiseled hieroglyphs onto tablets and Aristotle formulated his treatise on the proper ways to write a tragedy, prose and poetry have been tyrannized by strict rules of linguistics and form. It was probably when an ancient Sumerian scribe chiseled the wrong hieroglyph onto his stone tablet that he accidentally invented the metaphor. Ironically, the standards regarding what makes a great work of literature are fluid, ebbing and flowing from one generation of scholars and poets to the next. Grammar varies among languages. The conditions for proper written work are therefore utterly relative. Order within literature, then, is just a creation of mankind's vanity.

The traditional standards of literature have also led to a sectarian divide between an elite group of writers whose work has been deemed by relative standards to be worthy of publication against a vast majority of peasant-writers who have been oppressed and enslaved. Stories and poems that defy the standards of an authority naturally belong to the New New Ultra Weird.

The New New Ultra Weird, in its most characterized form, has attracted a new wave of brand new writers who might be labeled "amateurs" by traditional critics, but many public readers have come to accept as avante garde writers. The mind of an amateur is liberated from conventions and rules. It is a genre utterly and completely unique, for it is the only one that can be written most skillfully by those who have absolutely no idea what they are doing. There no "bad" writers anymore. Everyone is a brilliant surrealist.

Consider Eliyzabeth Yanne Strong-Anderson's theological dissertation, *BIRTH CONTROL IS SINFUL IN THE CHRISTIAN MARRIAGES AND IS ALSO ROBBING GOD OF PRIESTHOOD CHILDREN.* In her 648-page essay, the author experiments with form to augment the rhetoric of the piece. Normally, the reader's eye could hardly stand to read one paragraph written in all-caps, but Strong-Anderson composed her book exclusively in the uppercase. Carets, greater-than symbols, and other such punctuation are sprinkled throughout her prose, endowing the text with its own style and rhythm. Its narrator assumes the voice of God, and as a work of fiction it fits right in to the surrealist genre.

Sometimes it is the grammar which a writer will challenge, other times it is the subtler doctrines of aesthetics that an author puts to the test. The fantasy writer Ron Miller and his book *Silk and Steel* is a perfect example. Whereas George Martin might limit himself to one, perhaps a second metaphor in a paragraph, Miller washes his pages in the sheer beauty of his description. Carefully, instead of creating a ridiculous rant of conflicting images (as some stubborn critics have dared say!) he has mastered the art of enrapturing the reader with a single image, a single detail with its beauty for the illusion of eternity. The master of metaphor, Miller was even praised by Arthur C. Clarke for his craft.

THE OLD WEIRD

The appellation of the New New Ultra Weird has its strongest influence from an older movement, *The New Weird*, a genre closely resembling slipstream except most of its stories have been apparently retrieved from fanzines and blogs. In fact, the New Weird stories were so ~~terrible~~ innovative that they also are exemplary specimens of our own brand new genre, the New New Ultra Weird!

"The Neglected Garden," by Kathe Koja, a "weird" story that challenges the standards of proper characterization. Clearly the protagonist's girlfriend, pivotal to his suffering, needs no explained emotional motive for crucifying herself to a fence, or any explanation as to her hideous transformation into a tree demon (whether it be practical or symbolic). Such clarification is unnecessary, mere expositional drivel that would destroy the marketable strangeness of the piece.

Then there's Thomas Ligotti's short story, "A Soft Voice Whispers Nothing." His work was marveled and praised and even anthologized in *The New Weird*. The story is truly breathtaking, a tale of suicide and long rambling monologues, starring a character who is flatter than paper, and a setting filled with sights more baffling than disturbing as well as void of depth beyond flagrant Lovecraftian imitation. Most of all, it is about absolutely nothing, and nothing actually happens, conveyed cunningly by the title.

Jeffrey Thomas's "Immolation" exhibits striking parallels to *Bladerunner*: a futuristic setting completely overrun by Asian culture, dark, gritty, and focuses upon clones manufactured by corporations, a story that explores class differences and the strength of one lower-caste character to rise up against the oppressive "birthers." As a matter of fact, it's just like it. Yet why always the demand for originality? If audiences loved the same idea once, surely they'll love having the exact same old idea crammed down their throats ten million times.

Suffice to say, the New Weird paved the way for the New New Ultra Weird.

A Proto-Genre
The New New Ultra Weird has identifiable attributes that may be the start of a new genre, or else they could simply be the evolution of a psychological/literary effect that spans across all genres. Borges, the famous Latin American writer of magical realism, said every

writer creates his own precursors. It is a trend for writes of the New New Ultra Weird, then, to also create their own craft.

John Clute, author of the Encyclopedia of Science Fiction, says of science fiction that it "abandons the assumption that the world can be seen whole, and described accurately with words." The New New Ultra Weird, while not a subgenre of science fiction but rather its descendent, takes this concept to a whole new level. Some of its writers identify themselves as science fiction writers, such as Courtney and Theis, while many also have thrown away genre as a meaningless concept. In fact, one might claim that the New New Ultra Weird includes stories from every "genre," since stories of its nature are interstitial and defy categorization from both scholarly authority and market forces.

But it is acknowledged that you cannot define a genre simply by what it is not. Therefore, we will make a list of things that it is, or could be, or really should be if we have anything to say about it:

1. Awesome
2. Cool
3. Deep

That's it! Three simple abstractions make this an all-inclusive, instead of an exclusive, genre. The New New Ultra Weird is a genre for the layman, the commoner, your Average Joe, while still retaining aesthetic qualities. Because why should literature be beyond the capacity of the plumber down the street?

THE REVOLUTION

Criticism, of course, has arisen against this genre. Readers with lesser critical analysis abilities will assume works generated from the New New Ultra Weird movement to be absurd beyond any worthwhile interpretation. They might even go so far as to declare that this is all just "horrible writing" by novices and madmen and is just one huge joke on the publishing market. These people are morons. Do not listen to any of them.

The goal of this new genre is to subvert the pretense of interpretation. Once a reader or viewer is able to observe a work of art and gain absolutely nothing from the experience, THAT is the moment one is liberated from destructive bias and ambition. Our stories are not constrained to setting. They are not constrained to character. They are not constrained to tropes of genre. In fact, the New New Ultra Weird is not bound by any conventions at all. For it is only in the absence of conventions that the reader can begin to build conventions for himself.

The New New Ultra Weird, as noted by the Texan philosopher Gary Busey[3], is a genre that is even beyond post-modernism in its attempt to dismantle all assumptions created in society. It is even more powerful than the post-structural movement in deconstructing the binary oppositions of good and evil, black and white, truth and lies. A story can be said to have its origins in the nexus-ideas of the New New Ultra Weird if the purpose of its structure is to demonstrate solely that there is no such thing as structure, and that all meaning is meaningless. In response to the rising of this genre, Gary Busey attached the following antecdote in his latest book *Everyone Listen to Donald Trump!* : "Have a mind that's open to everything. Get attached to nothing."

Consider that episode of *Futurama* when Bender wants to become a cook, but because he's a robot, he has no sense of taste and his food causes most people a lethal case of reverse peristalsis. What Spargle told him demonstrates the vital core of the New New Ultra Weird: "Without the distraction of taste, your mind is free to touch the Zen of pure flavour. You could become the greatest chef ever." Beethoven was deaf, yet composed beautiful symphonies. Rembrandt was blind and had wooden hands, but that did not stop him from painting. The stories we've compiled in this anthology were written by authors with no taste, and therefore have unlimited potential for style, form, and plot.

As Gary Busey once said, "Art is a process; it is not the final

---

3. Specifically concerning his long-debated ethnicity, Gary Busey has this to say: "I consider myself a Texan. I grew up in Texas and Oklahoma."

form." His wisdom rings in the heart of the new wave of writers who march under the banner of the New New Ultra Weird. It is the spirit of the writer, not his product, which must be judged for its aesthetic value. This is the end to which all art has striven. In the world of literature, we have reached the end of history.

THIS ANTHOLOGY

Think of this anthology as a time machine, a device beyond your comprehension and yet believable, to travel through time to the "moment" that the New New Ultra Weird occurred, and we, your faithful editors, shall be your guide. Perhaps that moment hasn't occurred—maybe it will never occur.

This book begins with several works we believe to be the catalysts of the New New Ultra Weird moment, which includes both published and unpublished examples. We introduce the section with the poems of Amanda McKittrick Ros, followed by New New Ultra Weird science fiction writer Dale M. Courtney and the fantasy writer Jim Theis. Our intentions are that these works would represent the bulk of the wave of stories that first caught the attention of the public reader to the New New Ultra Weird, and have now become the building blocks of this publishing market. Think of it as an ode to these writers who started this literary movement without even knowing it.

In the "Vomitorium[4]," we have compiled a litany of fresh stories published only recently in magazines by new writers, many of whom have never been anthologized before. These writers have been educated (well, technically, *de*-educated) and have written with the awareness of the New New Ultra Weird.

After that we have the "Confabulation," an exact transcription of the internet debate which has set in stone some of the core vitals of the genre, yet still makes discussion of its finer details not only possible but intellectually ravishing, a sort of game between minds. Many popular voices of both the publishing and the commercial

---

4. NOT the place where ancient Romans would throw up food to make room for more (a popular misconception) but a series of entrance and exit passages in an ancient Roman theatre.

world added their own two cents, some you may be surprised to see. Several essays from different authors and editors following, giving us their insight on the New New Ultra Weird.

This anthology may be difficult to grasp at first. We ask that you open your mind, and you will see that there is no such thing as a bad writer. Just writers who are fresh and honest, maybe a little unorthodox. Because shouldn't there be room for everyone in the publishing market? Shouldn't EVERYONE in the world to be given the chance to fulfill a dream, to publish as many books as they can scribble on napkins or pound onto smartphones, even if they are completely illegible, unintelligent, banal, and vain?

I'm sure you will agree.

THE NEW NEW ULTRA WEIRD

VERSE
AMANDA McKITTRICK ROS

"The Lawyer" from _Poems of Puncture_
Beneath me here in stinking clumps
Lies Lawyer Largebones, all in lumps;
A rotten mass of clockholed clay,
Which grown more honeycombed each day.
See how the rats have scratched his face?
Now so unlike the human race;
I very much regret I can't assist them in their eager 'bent'

"Visiting Westminster Abbey" from _Fumes of Formation_
Holy Moses! Have a look!
Flesh decayed in every nook!
Some rare bits of brain lie here,
Mortal loads of beef and beer,
Some of whom are turned to dust,
Every one bids lost to lust;
Royal flesh so tinged with 'blue'
Undergoes the same as you.

THE NEW NEW ULTRA WEIRD

MOON PEOPLE, AN EXCERPT
DALE M. COURTNEY

Dale M. Courtney works for National Security on the part of foreign policies, war strategy, and global economic equality, and has served as an adviser for Presidents Bush and Obama. An astrologer and avid fisherman, Dale is a native of Miami Florida, having grown up during the Muriel flotilla of refugees from Cuba. He also served in the Army and toured Korea for a year. Moon People is set to be a film by 2016, directed by J. J. Abrams and starring Harrison Ford. To all of his readers Dale says, "Thank you and may God Bless your life."

one—THE BEGINNING OF THE END

This Story Begins on a beautiful sunny day in Daytona Beach Florida with a man by the name of David Braymer. A 45-year-old single man that works at the local high school as a science teacher. He also teaches astronomy in the 12- grade level. Now he has been here about 5 years and has become somewhat partial to a young lady by the name of Cheral Baskel a local restaurant owner in Daytona Beach Florida. At the moment, Cheral is preparing her restaurant for another shuttle launch at the cape. Everyone always gathers at her place because you can see the launch real good there. It is on the water and its real close to the Cape. She always decks the place out right before a launch too. Now David always goes to Cheral's place before work every morning for breakfast because it is on his way to his school. He has never missed a shuttle launch at Cherals place since he's been at his school. David was not always a teacher. Before he was a teacher, he use to work for the government for UFO. research about five years ago. He didn't like the job that much because he was always bored.

He really wanted to teach anyway. Today is also Oct.27 in the year 2048. The next shuttle launch at the Cape is on Halloween. There has been some unusual events the last 2 shuttle launches though. They would get right up to the launch sequence and stop the launch for some kind of weird problem.

Now everyone is very suspicious about the next launch on the 31 because of it being Halloween. They have also been launching three shuttles a week. Most of the people going back and forth on the shuttles are workers working on the three huge mobile base stations orbiting the Earth. Two of which are just about finished. They have also been trying to get David to join the crew on the U.S.S. Lunar Base 1 for about 2 years. Which is one of the base stations that is almost completed? However, he declines gracefully because he's a little scared of the launch process, Plus he likes the school he's at. Everybody laugh's about the way the base stations look. They look like a giant empty toilet paper holder from Earth, with one huge engine on the back of it. From in front of the engine to the front of the base station on the inside are all docking bays. There's ten stories' from top to bottom and all three base stations are a mile in diameter and about 2 miles long. They constantly rotate when they are in operation. The U.S.S. Lunar Base (1) and (2) are rotating at this time, and in about 3 months Lunar Base (3) will start rotating. The reason why they want David is his knowledge of the stars. Also because he worked for U.F.O. research.

They pay the workers a lot of money to work on the base stations and he would be an officer if he did decide to join the U.S.S. Lunar Base (1). First it starts on its mission to Mars for 6 month& Then off to Saturn's Moon Titan. The U.SS. Lunar Basa (2) it will first go to Venus for a year. Then it will head to Pluto and its moon's. U.S.S. Lunar Base (3) will go first to Jupiter for a year and then go to the outer parts of our solar system and beyond. They are also paying big money to either go to our Moon base and our Ma(s base to work for a ten year period. Now on this day David is on his way to the restaurant like always listening to his radio. His favorite song is playing when there's a interruption in the broadcast on die Emergency Broadcast System this is K92 FM we take you live to NASA with a special report. This is Steve Slader live on channel 9. Ladies and gentleman today NASA observatory has spotted a huge meteor headed toward Earth at a high rate of speed.

Coming very close. However. NASA officials believe that it will not hit Earth. It appears to be the size of a small Moon. They are also concerned about it hitting the Sun or our Moon. They believe if it hits any other planet we should be all right but NASA experts need to do some more studies and urge everyone not to panic. We're not sure about anything yet. What we do know is. it's coming from the direction of the constellation of Scorpio at the tail area. heading this way going approximately 60'OOO miles an hour and it is a planet killer! We repeat please do not panic. now we resume to your regular programming. David was thinking to himself Oh my God, this is unbelievable. I can't believe this! Could this be the end of us all that everyone predicted? I wonder if Cheral heard it on the news at the restaurant.

As David pulls in to Cheral's place.he sees many of the regular locals parked in the parking lot like normal. As he gets out of the car, he also notices everyone inside looks normal. As he conies through the door Cheral comes over with a big smile on her face. Hi stranger. as she looks at David's face she realizes something 15 "Tong. Then Cheral says, you look like you've just seen a ghost. What's wrong?

David took the worried look off of his face and answered, you haven't heard the news yet have you? No Cheral replied. I just got done in the kitchen and came out and seen you. Why what's wrong? Then David said, it's really nothing to panic about. Well, I just heard something on the radio just minutes ago. They said that there was a big meteor coming right at us from die constellation of Scorpio. Yeah sure thais real funny. Ha Ha. Then David said, no really Cheral I'm not kidding! Turn on your TV. There should be something on there now. I'll bet it's on every station. Cheral looks at David kind of funny and looks over at one of her regulars sitting by die TV and said bill can you turn on the TV that's behind you for me? Bill answered, sure for you anything. Then Cheral said could you put it on channel 9 please? Sure Bill answered. Then on came die TV.

The reporter Steve Slader was talking about the meteor. NASA reports were saying the meteor is increasing in speed. It appears that the meteor is going 69,000 miles an hour and is climbing in speed at the rate of 1,000 miles an hour every 6 hours. This is Steve

Slader. I take von live to NASA observatory to talk to Herbert Larson head astronomer. (Herbert Larson) At approximately 3:55 AM this morning we spotted a giant meteor in the constellation of Scorpio coming in our direction, At the current rate of speed, it should be here in about 178 Days.

Now we believe it's going to miss us by about 25000 miles. Its going to be real close, we will be following it very closely. We have experts on this all over the world. Everyone right now is busy trying to calculate where the meteor is going and if it will hit us when it arrives, for the next 178 days. Lady's and gentleman hopefully with God's help nothing will go Tong and we will see the most spectacular event the world has ever seen since the beginning of time. We'll be giving you more information as soon as we know more. Please it's very important not to panic it won't help at all. It will only make things worse.

Now we take you back to your regular programming. Now when David came in before everyone knew, it sounded like a regular restaurant with regular restaurant noises. As the reporter started telling everyone what was going on you could hear a mouse burp. Then at the end of the report you heard everyone say the same three words. "Oh my God". About half the people immediately got up with a terrified look on their face and said we have to go, and they paid their tab and left. Then one of Cheral's regular customers in the other half said I'm not going to panic. Hell, it might not even come close to us. Then David said, it would probably collide with something way before it comes near us. I'm going to go ahead and eat. I'm not going to panic either. Then everyone realized who David was and what he did for a living. Then everyone started to calm down and listened to what he was saying. Suddenly everybody went ahead and ate their breakfast. David turned to Cheral with a smile and Cheral said 222? David said you know me. yes maani. Coming right up Cheral replied. She had a sexy smile on her face and then went to the kitchen. David grabbed the newspaper and sat down at his usual booth and started reading the paper.

In no time, one of Cheral's waitresses came out with his breakfast. David ate pretty quickly. He put five dollars on the table and went over to the door of Cheral's kitchen and smiled.

He looked at Cheral and said, that was one good breakfast. That was sure quick Cheral replied. Then David said, yeah I know. You know what? I've been coming here for a long time and you know we never really got to know each other that well.

Do you think maybe that. David seemed to be a little nervous? Well I was wondering if you would like to go out with me some time? Cheral put a sexy smile on her face and said, you know I would really like that a lot. David put a big smile on his face. That's treat how about Friday ninht? Cheral said, ok that sounds good to me. Super David answered. I'll see you on Friday then. He said bye and 'went on to school. As he was driving to work he notice everyone seem to be driving a little crazy and yelling at each other. When he got to school, he notice everyone was running around panicking. Everybody was telling everyone to calm down, When he got to his room and got settled in. A couple of his best students Billy Berenson and Cathy Rigby arrived. They were a little panicked and asked David. Mr.

Braymer did you hear the news? Sure David replied. I'm going to hook up my new telescope and we will all watch it as it gets close. This is a special telescope that can see during the day.

It is one of the latest telescopes out. Their expensive but they work well. You can hook it up to your computer and watch it on your monitor. With our new chalk board size class computer monitors, we can watch it real good in the classroom, and its high definition too. All you need is the correct coordinates Then Billy said. that's pretty cool professor. Yeah that is cool Cathy replied! David spoke up and said I've got to go to the office to get some forms. I will be right back so be good. Billy and Cathy both said, O.k. Mr. Braymer. As David arrived at the office.

Everyone was very busy and a little panicky. It was close to chaos. He went over to the principal's office and walked in. The principal Mike Lever looked at David an said I'm glad you're here. I just received a phone call this morning from NASA. Asking about you and wanting to talk to you. They said it was pretty important. They gave me a number for you to call. I tried to find out what it was about but he wouldn't tell me. I'll bet it has something to do with the meteor doesn't it? I don't know David answered. I'll call and find out and let you know.

David went ahead and got his forms and went back to class. When he got back most of his students were starting to arrive. Everyone was kind of loud so he told everyone to calm down and please sit down. Everyone start studying his or her books for Friday's test I have to make a phone call and I'll be right back. David went to the teachers break room and called the number. Hello. NASA operations Bud Walker speaking. Yes how are you doing, my name is David Braymer, I am a 12th grade teacher at New Smyrna Beach High School. I was told someone was wanting to talk to me and that it was important.

TWO—THE NEW JOB

'YES, MR. BRAYMER. I'm head of operations out here at NASA. I was wondering if you were still active in the field of astronomy? Yes. David answered.

This is about the meteor isn't it? Yes Bud replied, I hear you're the best at what you do. David smiled and said. well I don't know about being the best. But I do teach astronomy in high school and I have been into astrology for about 20 years. Then Bud said. yes I know Mr. Braymer. Well I'm just going to come right out with it. Our head astronomer Herbert Lawson and his assistant were in a automobile accident yesterday. They're both in pretty bad shape. They will be all right but that gave us some empty positions we have to fill immediately. Because of our meteor that's coming right at us the last calculation shows and there's something else. Then David said. wait I have a job! Yes, I know Bud replied. We are willing to o the extra mile here. We will pay top dollar on this one and we have a substitute to take your place at school. All this is coming straight from the top. Mr. Braymer we need you real bad. We will also help you out with any other problem you might have.

David answered. well I don't know. I guess it all depends on one thing. Then Bud said. what's that? What was that something else you were talking about a minute ago, when you were talking about the meteor? You said there was something else. I can't tell you until you take the job. Bud replied. Then David said, can I have a little time to think about it first. Bud answered. Yes, you have until 5 o'clock today. David said. wow that's not much time. Yes I know Bud said, we can't help it the meteor isn't giving us much choice. Please all I ask is for you to think about it and give me a call later today. Ok sir I'll do that David answered. I'll give you a call either way Mr. Walker and then David said have a good day sir. Then David hung up and vent back to class. Then he arrived back to class he notice that half of his class "-as absent and the other half was playing around. All right, everyone sit down, David said. Let's get class going. Billy spoke up and said. does this mean we don't have to come to school because of the meteor. No, you should come to class unless someone says not to. David said. Then Cathy said no one else is. I know but we should still come unless they say otherwise. David replied. Now everyone open their astronomy books to page 286 to the constellation of Scorpio. This is what we are going to study for a couple of days. We will have a test on this Friday. I will also hook this telescope up to our new 80 inch chalk board computer monitor. This ought to be pretty cool once we set it up. Then everyone started studying and David started putting it all together. After about 30 minutes he had it all hooked up and was starting to turn everything on. Suddenly the monitor came on. David started adjusting the telescope to the constellation Scorpio and finally it came in so good it seemed like it was night.

The hole class made a wow sound and then they all said about the same time" cool". At that point David knew he had a hit, then he told Billy to turn out the class room lights. They could see die meteor as clear as night time also everyone shouted out there it is, wow! Look at that picture. David said that's pretty good high definition, It's so clear. The whole class at the same time said yeah! The meteor was coming from the end of the tail section. 'iiere die stinger is in the constellation of Scorpio.

Then Cathy said, Mr. Braymer how's the high definition come in so good, its broad daylight? This is one of the latest telescopes out David said, when you use it in the daytime it mixes with our Hubble

7 satellite telescope in space. That's how it zooms in so close and so clear. That is a good picture, and it looks so close. This is better than I thought! Vait a minute that's not coming from Lambda Scorpio off die stinger that's coming from An tares region but that's over *135* million light years away, there's no way that could get here in one hundred and seventy eight days. I wonder who did the calculations on that?

Boy they do need help! Wait a minute. I should be able to calculate die speed thanks to my new telescope called Zeus- Then David said, Zeus can you locate and lock in on the meteor that is moving told us at a high rate of speed in the constellation of Scorpio? (Zeus) Affirmative, "Located." Cool. the whole class said out loud again. You could see Zeus zoom in on the meteor. Then David said, Zeus can you calculate the speed and size of the meteor coming from the An tares star system, coming to our solar system? Affirmative, one moment please. Meteor is coming approximately 182,000 kilometers an hour and increasing speed 5,005 kilometers every 24 hours. Meteor is ten kilometers in diameter. Vow the class sounded out!

David asked, Zeus how long before the meteor enters our solar system? (Zeus) Meteor will be entering into your solar system in approximately 204 days 6 hours 22 minutes and 44 seconds. Wow the class sounded out! Billy looks at David and yelled out, ask Zeus if the meteor is going to hit Earth. David thought about it for a moment and said maybe I shouldn't The whole class yells out, why not? Billy tells David hey professor we are all in this together. It's not that simple Billy, David replied. The computer could be off I just hooked it up.

Three—The Unknown

THERE'S A LOT OF THINGS that could be wrong and everyone would leave here and go start a panic all over the place. Billy said, Ah we won't tell anyone. I don't think I can take that chance David replied. Then Billy said, how about if we all pledge not to say anything? David smiled and thought for a moment and said, this is serious people, a lot of people can die in a panic. We will really give our word Billy

THE NEW NEW ULTRA WEIRD

said, won't we class? Yeah the class sounded out! David laughed and said, ok listen very carefully class. If you here by pledge to this class and to God that you will not tell anyone what we find out in this class about the meteor. I will ask Zeus that question. Everyone has to say I do though. Everybody in the class sounded out, I do. I hope I'm not making a big mistake? Ok Zeus will this meteor collide with any planet in our solar system? (Computer) Negative. There is a 94% possibility that it will collide with your star. The whole class went silent. Then David said, remember people I just hooked this up it may not be accurate. Zeus, is there a chance that it won't hit our sun? Affirmative, there is a 6% chance that the meteor won't hit your star. Zeus do a system check. (Zeus) Affirmative. Zeus is now doing a systems check. A 30 second pause. System check complete, Zeus is functioning at 100 % effectiveness.

The class went silent again and then the bell rang. Remember class don't say anything about what you have heard David said, people can die panicking. You took a pledge. Billy answered, don't worry professor we won't say anything. Then David said, ok I am going to trust you then. There's still a big chance that it won't hit anything. We know doc, Billy answered. There's a six percent chance. We'll see you later professor. David grinned and said smarty pants, Ok, good bye. Then Billy laughed and walked out with Cathy and finally all the students cleared out of the room, all of which had a doom look on their face. David thought about it for a minute and decided to make the call. Hello Mr. Walker, this is David Braymer. Bud answered, yes how's it going. Well Mr. Braymer what's it going to be. I believe I'm going to take the job David said. That's great Bud replied. Then David said, by the way sir, what were you talking about earlier? I'll tell you when you get here, Bud said. Ok David answered, I'll go ahead and make your arrangements here for a substitute and I'll come on down. I will notify the gate that you are coming, Bud replied. Very good sir, David said. I will see you in a little while. David went ahead and made arrangements at the office for a substitute and then headed out to NASA. When David finally arrived at NASA, he had forgotten how big NASA had gotten in the past few years. David then found Bud walkers office and went in.

As David was walking in, Bud was walking out and almost bumped into each other. Hey, there he is, Bud said. Then David said, I finally made it. Good Bud replied, why don't you join me and I will take you on a tour to operations real quick. Ok David said. Boy NASA is really getting pretty big isn't it? Bud answered. yes every since we started building these base stations NASA has really gotten huge. David asked. Bud what were you talking about on the phone that you couldn't tell inc about? Are you ready for this, Bud asked? Yes I am David said. Then Bud said, here goes. We are still checking but it looks like our meteor has changed direction not once but two times in the past two weeks. David asked. what are you saying? You mean you're saying it's a spacecraft? No sir Bud said. I'm only telling you what I know. There's something else. David said what? Bud answered, the meteor was going 64,000 miles an hour and then all of our instruments indicated it increased its speed to double in less than 10 minutes. It's also ten kilometers in diameter. David said, that's incredible. Bud replied, yeah I know I said the same thing. Then David said, so what's everyone speculating? Vel1 it goes from one thing to another, Bud said. One person says maybe the reason that the meteor changed direction was from bumping into some kind of an object in space that we can't see. However, that does not explain the increase in speed. In addition. the other side of the coin is that it is some kind of an alien spaceship. However, what we do know is that it is ten kilometers in size and now on the present course, it is going to hit our sun. Then David said, I tell you though if someone were going to visit us, they would probably set a course for the star in that system. I never thought of that, said Bud. If they are aliens. I wonder what they want with us.

David told Bud. you know our planet must look pretty good from 135 million light years away. Then Bud said man I tell yeah this meteor sure does look eerie on the telescope. David said. yes I know I have a Zeus telescope system hooked up in my classroom and it practically terrified my class.

It said the same thing yours said. Oh, no, I do not see how we are going to stop a panic if everyone is watching on his or her new telescope. Bud replied.

Then David said, yeah I know what you're saying. Well here we are, Bud said. I would like to introduce you to your new assistant Mr. Kim Moon. How do you do Nir. Moon. David asked? Pretty good Kim replied. I'm a little tired, but I'll be all right. How are you? Mr. Moon Bud said I am putting David Braymer in charge of all operations on the meteor. If you have anything new on the meteor tell this man right here.

FOUR—THE JOB OFFER

HE IS YOUR NEW BOSS here on out. David you report to me. Yes sir, David answered. Then Bud said Mr. Moon will you show Mr. Braymer around and update him on everything new? Yes sir, it would be my pleasure replied Kim. Ok good luck, then Bud went back to his office. Kim spoke up and said follow me. I will show you everything there is to know Mr. Braymer. Just call me David. Ok just call me *Mr.* Moon. No, I'm kidding just call me Kim. Ok Mr. Kim. No just Kim will be tine. Gotcha. David replied. David smiled at Kim. well Mr. Moon what's your assessment of this meteor? Kim looked over at his assistant Martin and said Martin would you put the meteor on the main viewer. Yes, sir answered Martin. Well David said Kim, sir I would have to say at the moment there's not enough data but one thing is for sure we are going to find out because it's coming right at us. In addition, it's ten kilometers wide. Yes. I know. David said.

We were tracking it at our school. This satellite system makes our new system at school look like a toy.

Then Kim said, it should because this is the best telescope system in the world. As they. were both looking at the viewer at the same time? There was a sudden flash of light and the meteor suddenly vanished. What happened. David asked? I do not know, Kim replied. Martin do a system check. I'm on it Martin answered. Then Kim said, let me check a few things here. Im just going to zoom in on our friend. Suddenly the screen zoomed in but there was still no sign of the meteor. Did it explode? There were large amounts of radiation all around the area. Kim was asking himself. There doesn't seem to be any debris anywhere, it's as if it just vanished. Well maybe we don't have to worry about the meteor any more. (David) Wow maybe.

(Kim) Let's keep after it and do some more studies. Wait did you see that? (David) Yeah. that second flash. Yes. Kim replied., look how far away that was from where the meteor was last reported. Then David said.. do you think that was the meteor? Kim answered. I do not know. Let me look at something real quick. Just as I thought. That flash of light was on the same heading as our meteor was on when it disappeared. But in order for it to get to this point, this quick it would have to be doing an excess of about 300.000 miles an hour. Wow, that's incredible! (David) Yeah do you think that's the meteor? That flash of light. (Kim) I don't know it sure does look funny. We will keep watching it. If it flashes again and it's on the same course, we'll know something's up. Then David said, I'm going to infonu Bud of what's going on. Sure Kim said. I'm going to do some more checking and I'll get back to you. Ok David replied. I'll use this phone. Bud answered hello. David spoke up Bud, it's me David Braymer. I already have a report to make. It is kind of great news. Then Bud said, oh yeah what is it?

Well it seems our meteor has vanished off the charts in one big flash of light David said. Are you kidding me Bud asked? No. I'm not replied David. We also could not find any debris either. Except large amounts of radiation and there's one more thing. We also seen a flash of light 1 light year away. Three minutes after the meteor vanished. It was on the same heading our meteor was on. (Bud) Wow, all that just happened?

I just left you 5 minutes ago. Man there's all kind of stuff happening today. (David) Yes, I know Kim and I was just watching the big view screen when it happened right in front of us. We are watching to see if there are any more flashes of light even further down the same heading as our meteors heading. (Bud) Why what's everyone speculating? (David) We're not sure yet. Nevertheless, it may be the ends of all of our problems. Then Bud said Boy, wouldn't that be a load off of everybody? Oh yes, David before I go I wanted to talk to you about something very important.

Oh. what's that, David asked? (Bud) Well I just got off the phone with the White House. We've got orders to get these base stations on their way with their missions with a full crew and supplies. I have another Job offer for you. (David) Oh really what's that? (Bud) 'We need a 1st Science Officer and navigator, and also a astronomer for U.S.S. Lunar Base 1. The pay is excellent. You would have the rank of Captain. You would be under the command of Admiral Benson. Now I know him personally and not only is he pretty sharp. He's also a great guy to work under. However, it is long term. It doesn't get any rawer than this it takes a special kind of man to do something like this but if you have the stones, we've got the job for you. Then David said, this is quite an offer. I've always wanted to do something like this. I was offered this a couple of years ago but I turned it down. I didn't think it was for me. However, I never in a thousand years thought that I ever would do it for real. (Bud) Well think it over. I've got to make a decision quick so let me know within the next couple of days until then, you can run operations on the meteor project.

Five—The Big One

KEEP ME INFORMED could yeah. (David) It would be my pleasure sir. (Bud) I'll catch you later. (David) Yes, sir I'll keep you informed and I'll let you know about the job to. Have a good one. David hung up the phone and started to stare at the large monitor. Kim walked over to David and said what did Bud say about the meteors' (David) He couldn't believe it. He also offered me the position of First Science Officer aboard the Lunar Base 1. (Kim) Wow, what did you tell him? (David) That I don't know and I would have to think on it. Hey maybe we shouldn't tell anyone about all this yet. Ok' (Kim) Gauche. I've been watching the monitor and I haven't seen any more flashes. It just seems to have vanished. I also alerted the computer to tell us if there are any more flashes of light anywhere on the heading that our meteor was on before it vanished. (David) 7e11 maybe it is no longer a problem anymore. Nevertheless, we will keep on watching just the same.

You never know any more. Hopefully it will just go down in history as a big scare. Suddenly the phone rings its Bud.

Hey, David I have the press all over me here. I am going to have to tell them something. Have there been any more flashes of light or anything else to talk about? Can we say we are out of danger yet?

What do you think? (David) Bud so far we have not seen any other phenomenon in the area and everything looks nonnal. I have to say it does look like we might be out of the woods. I guess I would tell them that, and that we will keep on watching the area just to be sure but everything at the moment looks great. (Bud) Ok that is what I am going to say then. Hey, don't forget to let inc know about that job. (David) You got it. I'll call you in the next 2 days or I'll be here. and I'll let you know. (Bud) All right, I'm going to go ahead and go. I have some stuff I have to get down. I'll see you later. (David) All right. see you tomorrow sir. Hey Kim if you want, let's go ahead and keep and eye on that meteor's heading. If you see another flash give me a call right away. I'm going to go ahead and leave. I have a lot of things to think about and do and very little time to do it in. (Kim) All right I'll see you in the morning. David went ahead and left and vent to his house in New Smyrna Beach. When he got there, he made himself a sandwich, sat down, and told his computer to turn on his T.V. There was already a news update on about the meteor disappearing. Everyone seemed like they were back to normal acting again. I wonder if I could just pick up and go? Man being a Captain on a base station would be really cool. There is a ten-year commitment though. Boy that's a long time. All of my students would probably think that it would be cool to have their teacher on a base station. I really don't have anything holding me down here except my class and they could live without me. You know I might just take that job. Bud said the job paid good and I bet it does.

It would sure beat what I'm making now. Maybe I should have taking the job hvo years ago. Its seems to be my destiny. You know I think I'll eat my sandwich and go to class and get a few things together. I'll take another look at Zeus. All of the students should be gone by now. David ate his sandwich and went back to school.

As he was arriving, everyone was just about gone for the day. He went in his room and turned on Zeus. He focused where the meteor was last sighted. He just started staring into space in deep thought for about 30 minutes.

You know most people live their whole life and never get a chance like this. I do love space and everything in it. I always have. I believe I am going to do it. I think I will take this job. David wrote a good-bye letter to his class and went home. The next morning David got up early and headed straight to Cherals restaurant. 'When he got there he sat down at his regular booth. Cheral walked right over and said hey stranger how's it going?

Real good David replied. You're not going to believe what all happened to me yesterday. (Cheral) Oh, what happened? (David) Well yesterday, NASA called me and needed me to help with the meteor so I took the job. Then they went ahead and offered me another job on the U.S.S. Lunar Base 1 as the 1st Science Officer. (Cheral) Wow, are you going to take it?

(David) I do not know. I think I might. I will never get a better offer than this. I always wanted to do something like this but I never thought I would ever get the opportunity. (Cheral) Isn't that a long-term commitment? (David) Yes it is. It's a ten—year commitment. (Cheral) Wow. that is long term. (David) What do you think I should do? (Cheral) I think you should do what your gut is telling you to do.

(David) My gut is telling me to do it. (Cheral) Then I think you should do it. (David) Do you still want to go out with me tomorrow? (Cheral) I wouldn't miss it for the world. Do you want your regular 222 (David) You bet.

SIX—THE crew

DAVID GRABBED THE PAPER and ate his breakfast. He told Cheral he would see her tomorrow night at seven and they would go out and eat somewhere. Cheral had a big smile on her face and said. that sounds great. David said I will see you then and went onto work. He finally arrived at operations at NASA and everyone was just changing shifts. Kim was just arriving too and said good morning. (David) Good morning, (Kim) I have already checked, there has not been any more flashes of light last night or our alarm would have went off. I guess we might be out of the woods. (David) I think we are too. (Kim) Well did you decide yet about the job on U.S.S. Lunar Base 1? (David) I think I am going to take it. (Kim) All right, I bet you will love that job. (David) I hope so because it is a ten-year commitment. The only thing I do not like about everything is that my shuttle goes off on October 31, which is Halloween. Kim smiled some and said you know you're right. I never thought of that. I think that would bother me to. (David) I am going to go ahead and call Bud and tell him the good news.

David calls Bud and Bud answers the phone. Hello. (David) Hey. it's me David Braymer, I just wanted to call and tell you that I have decided to take the job on U.S.S. Lunar Base 1. (Bud) Hey, that's great. You know they really need you aboard. You will have a good crew aboard the 1.J.S.S. Lunar Base I. Well I guess you need to talk to Admiral Benson. I will call hini in a couple of minutes and set everything up, and you can talk to him today sometime and you can make arrangements with him. He will probably want you to go and pack what you want to take with you and report to your new home, the Lunar Base 1. Hey, David let me get on this. I wiLl get back to you in a little while. (David) Ok I will catch you later. (Kim) Let me set up the lay out of Lunar Base 1 on the computer and you can check out your new home. It is actually a pretty elaborate space station it has everything on board that a small city has. Including a couple of bars on board and also a couple of shopping malls. A basket Ball court. There is even a small farm on board. You have everything there that you need. You are totally independent. (David) Cool, I will check this out. I might as well get to how my new home. As David went through the Lunar Base 1 program he realized that the base station did have a lot more extras than he thought. It did have everything a city has including a full size hospital and staff. It also has a 11111 size observatory. Vhich I cannot wait to take a look at. I will bet it is nicer than anything I am use to. Hey. look, here these ships even have weapons. We got a laser and missiles and rockets, wow. She is also very nicely decorated. and very classy looking too. Look here. this baby has got five shuttles also armed with lasers and rockets. All of a sudden, the phone rings. David answers the phone. hello. (Admiral Benson) Hello. Mr. Braymner this is Admiral Benson.

I was just told by Mr. Walker director of NASA that you have decided to take the job of 1St Science Officer aboard the U.S.S. Lunar Base 1. Is that true? (David) Yes. it is. I was hoping I would get to talk to you today about this. (Admiral Benson) Yes as soon as Bud told me about you. I called right away. Two of our crewmembers were hurt in an automobile accident, and we just got orders to leave space dock as soon as possible from the White House. In addition. we are not coming back for a very long time. Are you sure, you want to go? (David) Yes, sir I have made up my mind and there is no turning back now. (Admiral Benson) Ok then welcome aboard. The last shuttle takes off at 0900 On Monday morning. By the way did you realize that Monday was Halloween. (David) Yes, I know, it does bother me a little bit. (Admiral Benson) You have until then to change your mind. You are going to have to be here a good 24 hours earlier for launch preparations and a quick health check up. Then after that the only thing you are going to see is the stars. Don't worry I'll be there right alongside of you? That's my flight to. (David) Great. The truth about it is I am a little scared of that shuttle launch to the base station especially on Halloween. But I think I will be all right after that. (Admiral Benson) Good Captain Braymer because you amid I are going on one hell of a ride Monday morning, trick or treat. I will show you wonders you always dreamed about. (David) That's pretty cool sir. I can't wait. (Admiral Benson) Well then I'll see you around 0900 Sunday for launch preparations. Yes sir David answered. I'll see you then. (Admiral Benson) Ok. good-bye. David hung up the phone. He couldn't believe this was all happening so quick and that Monday morning he was going to leave earth for a very long time.

Kim was watching David and walked over and said, what's a matter you having second thoughts. (David) No not at all. I just cant believe how fast everything in going in my life. (Kim) Yeah I know what you mean. It isn't every day you leave Earth and go out into space. You know Bud offered that other assistant Science Officer job on Lunar Base 1 to me. (David). Hey that's great. Are you going to take it? (Kim) I don't know I'm sure thinking about it. I just might. The pay is great.

seven—FaTe sTeps in

THAT IS SURE A LONG TIME to have to leave Earth. (David) Yes I know,
but I've made up my mind and I'm going to do it. (Kim) I wish I could

be as sure as you are. (David) I guess I'm ready for a little excitement in my life before I get old and die. You only live once you know. (Kim) Yeah I know what you mean.

I've been here about 10 years and I have gotten use to coming in every day, But I have always wanted to leave on a big space mission. I only have my father to look after. He can take care of himself he don't really need me. Then David said. I'm also doing this because I know I will never get another chance as good as this one, that pays so well with the rank of Captain. You know I feel like I've been giving a second chance in life or live two different lives in two different dimensions. I can't wait to start it. Hey Kim there hasn't been any more flashes of light have there, on the same heading as our meteor was on. (Kim) No sir it looks like we seen the last of our meteor. Everything looks normal in that area of space. (David) You know that sure was weird how that vanished like that. (Kim) Yes I know.

I thought for sure we were going to see another flash of light on down the road on that same heading. I don't know why. I guess it was the way it disappeared. (David) Yes I guess I was kind of hoping that too, but you never really know. You know I've been looking at the U.S.S. Lunar Base 1 on the computer and this base stations got it all just like you said. This little venture may be better than I thought it would be. It's got all kinds of room on it. It says here that it can even come apart in three different independent working sections. In case one or two sections get damaged or destroyed. That's really incredible. I know I'm doing the right thing. Well I'll know if you changed your mind if I see you onboard. You know Kim it's already time to call it a day. Time has really been flying lately. At least it seems that way to me. Hey Kim I'll see you in the morning. Have a good evening. (Kim) You too boss. David went home the whole time he looked like he was in a trance or a state of euphoria.

When he got home he ate a quick sandwich and 'vent to bed. It's like he couldn't wait for tomorrow so he went ahead and went to sleep as fast as he could. The next morning he received a phone call it was Bud. Good morning, how's it going?

(David) Oh pretty good, is everything still on? (Bud) You bet. I just called to tell you not to come in today. Instead take today and

Saturday off and get everything in order. You might want to say good-bye to your friends or pack all your stuff you want to take with you. In addition, just bring it with you Sunday morning when you come for launch preparations. (David) Ok. no problem here. (Bud) Ok I will see you Sunday morning then. (David) Ok I ill see you then sir.

Then David hung up the phone and got dressed. Well I guess I will go eat some breakfast, go to the school and say goodbye to everybody. Then come home and pack. I guess I will go out to eat with Cheral tonight and then come home and do some more packing. When David arrived at Cheral's restaurant. Everything seemed to be business as usual. Just like it was before the meteor came and went. David sat down in his usual seat and Cheral came out when she seen David come in. Hey stranger how's it going? I've been keeping an eye out looking for you this morning. Are we still on for supper tonight? (David) You bet. I've had nothing else on my mind since we talked about it. I thought we might eat at Red Lobster in Daytona. Wait I don't even know if you like seafood. (Cheral) Don't worry I love seafood and I love Red Lobster, they have great food there. I haven't eaten there in about a year.

This is going to be great. Do you want the usual 222? I would love the 222, thank you. (Cheral) Coming right up. Hey Cindy would you get this man a cup of decafe please. (Cindy) Coming right up. I'll get you a paper too ok. (David) Sure thank you. It didit take long before Dave's breakfast was done. Cheral brought it out to him and told him that she had one more order to get out and she would come out and sit with him for a while. David said I would really like that, with a big smile on his face. He notice his breakfast was perfect looking. Then he said this breakfast looks good, thank you. Cheral had a big smile and said. any time. David went at it. When he was almost done with his breakfast. Cheral came out and sat down with David. David said this breakfast was delicious. thank you very much. (Cheral) I'm glad you liked it. Did you make tip your mind about the base station job? (David) Yes I did. I'm going to do it.

But what I didn't know was that I was going to go so quick. (Cheral) How quick? (David) I have to show up at 0900 Sunday morning for flight preparations and a quick health check up. Then we launch Monday morning on Halloween at 0900. (Cheral) Wow, that is quick.

The Eye of Argon
Jim Theis

In the words of the manuscript's transcriber, "No mere transcription can give the true flavor of the original printing. It was mimeographed with stencils cut on an elite manual typewriter. Many letters were so faint as to be barely readable, others were over-struck, and some that were to be removed never got painted out with correction fluid. Usually, only one space separated sentences, while paragraphs were separated by a blank line and were indented ten spaces. Many words were grotesquely hyphenated. And there were illustrations -- I cannot do them justice in mere words, but they were a match for the text."

one

The weather beaten trail wound ahead into the dust racked climes of the baren land which dominates large portions of the Norgolian empire. Age worn hoof prints smothered by the sifting sands of time shone dully against the dust splattered crust of earth. The tireless sun cast its parching rays of incandescense from overhead, half way through its daily revolution. Small rodents scampered about, occupying themselves in the daily accomplishments of their dismal lives. Dust sprayed over three heaving mounts in blinding clouds, while they bore the burdonsome cargoes of their struggling overseers.

"Prepare to embrace your creators in the stygian haunts of hell, barbarian", gasped the first soldier.

"Only after you have kissed the fleeting stead of death, wretch!" returned Grignr.

A sweeping blade of flashing steel riveted from the massive barbarians hide enameled shield as his rippling right arm thrust forth, sending a steel shod blade to the hilt into the soldiers vital organs. The disemboweled mercenary crumpled from his saddle and sank to the clouded sward, sprinkling the parched dust with crimson droplets of escaping life fluid.

The enthused barbarian swiveled about, his shock of fiery red hair tossing robustly in the humid air currents as he faced the attack of the defeated soldier's fellow in arms.

"Damn you, barbarian" Shrieked the soldier as he observed his comrade in death.

A gleaming scimitar smote a heavy blow against the renegade's spiked helmet, bringing a heavy cloud over the Ecordian's misting brain. Shaking off the effects of the pounding blow to his head, Grignr brought down his scarlet streaked edge against the soldier's crudely forged hauberk, clanging harmlessly to the left side of his opponent. The soldier's stead whinnied as he directed the horse back from the driving blade of the barbarian. Grignr leashed his mount forward as the hoarsely piercing battle cry of his wilderness bred race resounded from his grinding lungs. A twirling blade bounced harmlessly from the mighty thief's buckler as his rolling right arm cleft upward, sending a foot of blinding steel ripping through the Simarian's exposed gullet. A gasping gurgle from the soldier's writhing mouth as he tumbled to the golden sand at his feet, and wormed agonizingly in his death bed.

Grignr's emerald green orbs glared lustfully at the wallowing soldier struggling before his chestnut swirled mount. His scowling voice reverberated over the dying form in a tone of mocking mirth. "You city bred dogs should learn not to antagonize your better." Reining his weary mount ahead, grignr resumed his journey to the Noregolian city of Gorzam, hoping to discover wine, women, and adventure to boil the wild blood coarsing through his savage veins.

The trek to Gorzom was forced upon Grignr when the soldiers of Crin were leashed upon him by a faithless concubine he had wooed. His scandalous activities throughout the Simarian city had unleashed throngs of havoc and uproar among it's refined patricians, leading them to tack a heavy reward over his head.

He had barely managed to escape through the back entrance of the inn he had been guzzling in, as a squad of soldiers tounced upon him. After spilling a spout of blood from the leader of the mercenaries as he dismembered one of the officer's arms, he retreated to his mount to make his way towards Gorzom, rumoured

The New New Ultra Weird

to contain hoards of plunder, and many young wenches for any man who has the backbone to wrest them away.

TWO

Arriving after dusk in Gorzom,grignr descended down a dismal alley, reining his horse before a beaten tavern. The redhaired giant strode into the dimly lit hostelry reeking of foul odors, and cheap wine. The air was heavy with chocking fumes spewing from smolderingtorches encased within theden's earthen packed walls. Tables were clustered with groups of drunken thieves, and cutthroats, tossing dice, or making love to willing prostitutes.

Eyeing a slender female crouched alone at a nearby bench, Grignr advanced wishing to wholesomely occupy his time. The flickering torches cast weird shafts of luminescence dancing over the half naked harlot of his choice, her stringy orchid twines of hair swaying gracefully over the lithe opaque nose, as she raised a half drained mug to her pale red lips.

Glancing upward, the alluring complexion noted the stalwart giant as he rapidly approached. A faint glimmer sparked from the pair of deep blue ovals of the amorous female as she motioned toward Grignr, enticing him to join her. The barbarian seated himself upon a stool at the wenches side, exposing his body, naked save for a loin cloth brandishing a long steel broad sword, an iron spiraled battle helmet, and a thick leather sandals, to her unobstructed view.

"Thou hast need to occupy your time, barbarian",questioned the female?

"Only if something worth offering is within my reach." Stated Grignr,as his hands crept to embrace the tempting female, who welcomed them with open willingness.

"From where do you come barbarian, and by what are you called?" Gasped the complying wench, as Grignr smothered her lips with the blazing touch of his flaming mouth.

The engrossed titan ignored the queries of the inquisitive female, pulling her towards him and crushing her sagging nipples to his yearning chest. Without struggle she gave in, winding her soft arms around the harshly bronzedhide of Grignr corded shoulder blades, as his calloused hands caressed her firm protruding busts.

"You make love well wench," Admitted Grignr as he reached for the vessel of potent wine his charge had been quaffing.

A flying foot caught the mug Grignr had taken hold of, sending its blood red contents sloshing over a flickering crescent; leashing tongues of bright orange flame to the foot trodden floor.

"Remove yourself Sirrah, the wench belongs to me;" Blabbered a drunken soldier, too far consumed by the influences of his virile brew to take note of the superior size of his adversary.

Grignr lithly bounded from the startled female, his face lit up to an ashen red ferocity, and eyes locked in a searing feral blaze toward the swaying soldier.

"To hell with you, braggard!" Bellowed the angered Ecordian, as he hefted his finely honed broad sword.

The staggering soldier clumsily reached towards the pommel of his dangling sword, but before his hands ever touched the oaken hilt a silvered flash was slicing the heavy air. The thews of the savages lashing right arm bulged from the glistening bronzed hide as his blade bit deeply into the soldiers neck, loping off the confused head of his senseless tormentor.

With a nauseating thud the severed oval toppled to the floor, as the segregated torso of Grignr's bovine antagonist swayed, then collapsed in a pool of swirled crimson.

In the confusion the soldier's fellows confronted Grignr with unsheathed cutlasses, directed toward the latters scowling make-up.

"The slut should have picked his quarry more carefully!" Roared the victor in a mocking baritone growl, as he wiped his dripping blade on the prostrate form, and returned it to its scabbard.

"The fool should have shown more prudence, however you shall rue your actions while rotting in the pits." Stated one of the sprawled soldier's comrades.

Grignr's hand began to remove his blade from its leather housing, but retarded the motion in face of the blades waving before his face.

"Dismiss your hand from the hilt, barbarbian, or you shall find a foot of steel sheathed in your gizzard."

Grignr weighed his position observing his plight, where-upon he took the soldier's advice as the only logical choice. To attempt to hack his way from his present predicament could only warrant certain death. He was of no mind to bring upon his own demise if an alternate path presented itself. The will to necessitate his life forced him to yield to the superior force in hopes of a moment of carlessness later upon the part of his captors in which he could effect a more plausible means of escape.

"You may steady your arms, I will go without a struggle."

"Your decision is a wise one, yet perhaps you would have been better off had you forced death," the soldier's mouth wrinkled to a sadistic grin of knowing mirth as he prodded his prisoner on with his sword point.

After an indiscriminate period of marching through slinking alleyways and dim moonlighted streets the procession confronted a massive seraglio. The palace area was surrounded by an iron grating, with a lush garden upon all sides.

The group was admitted through the gilded gateway and Grignr was ledalong a stone pathway bordered by plush vegitation lustfully enhanced by the moon's shimmering rays. Upon reaching the palace the group was granted entrance, and after several minutes of explanation, led through several winding corridors to a richly draped chamber.

Confronting the group was a short stocky man seated upona golden throne. Tapestries of richly draped regal blue silk covered all walls of the chamber, while the steps leading to the throne were plated with sparkling white ivory. The man upon the throne had a naked wench seated at each of his arms, and a trusted advisor seated in back of him. At each cornwr of the chamber a guard stood at attention, with upraised pikes supported in their hands, golden chainmail adorning their torso's and barred helmets emitting scarlet plumes enshrouding their heads. The man rose from his throne to the dias surrounding it. His plush turquois robe dangled loosely from his chuncky frame.

The soldiers surrounding Grignr fell to their knees with heads bowed to the stone masonry of the floor in fearful dignity to their sovereign, leige.

"Explain the purpose of this intrusion upon my chateau!"

"Your sirenity, resplendent in noble grandeur, we have brought this yokel before you (the soldier gestured toward Grignr) for the redress or your all knowing wisdon in judgement regarding his fate."

"Down on your knees, lout, and pay proper homage to your sovereign!" commanded the pudgy noble of Grignr.

"By the surly beard of Mrifk, Grignr kneels to no man!" scowled the massive barbarian.

"You dare to deal this blasphemous act to me! You are indeed brave stranger, yet your valor smacks of foolishness."

"I find you to be the only fool, sitting upon your pompous throne, enhancing the rolling flabs of your belly in the midst of your elaborate luxuryand ..." The soldier standing at Grignr's side smote him heavily in the face with the flat of his sword, cutting short the harsh words and knocking his battered helmet to the masonry with an echo-ing clang.

The paunchy noble's sagging round face flushed suddenly pale, then pastily lit up to a lustrous cherry red radiance. His lips trembled with malicious rage, while emitting a muffled sibilant gibberish. His sagging flabs rolled like a tub of upset jelly, then compressed as he sucked in his gut in an attempt to conceal his softness.

The prince regained his statue, then spoke to the soldiers surrounding Grignr, his face conforming to an ugly expression of sadistic humor.

"Take this uncouth heathen to the vault of misery, and be sure that his agonies are long and drawn out before death can release him."

"As you wish sire, your command shall be heeded immediately," answered the soldier on the right of Grignr as he stared into the barbarians seemingly unaffected face.

The advisor seated in the back of the noble slowly rose and advanced to the side of his master, motioning the wenches seated at his sides to remove themselves. He lowered his head and whispered to the noble.

"Eminence, the punishment you have decreed will cause much misery to this scum, yet it will last only a short time, then release him to a land beyond the sufferings of the human body. Why not mellow him in one of the subterranean vaults for a few days, then send him to life labor in one of your buried mines.

To one such as he, a life spent in the confinement of the stygian pits will be an infinitely more appropiate and lasting torture."

The noble cupped his drooping double chin in the folds of his briming palm, meditating for a moment upon the rationality of the councilor's word's, then raised his shaggy brown eyebrows and turned toward the advisor, eyes aglow.

"...As always Agafnd, you speak with great wisdom. Your words ring of great knowledge concerning the nature of one such as he ," sayeth , the king. The noble turned toward the prisoner with a noticable shimmer reflecting in his frog-like eyes, and his lips contorting to a greasy grin. "I have decided to void my previous decree. The prisoner shall be removed to one of the palaces underground vaults. There he shall stay until I have decided that he has sufficiently simmered, whereupon he is to be allowed to spend the remainder of his days at labor in one of my mines."

Upon hearing this, Grignr realized that his fate would be far less merciful than death to one such as he, who is used to roaming the countryside at will. A life of confinement would be more than his body and mind could stand up to. This type of life would be immeasurably worse than death.

"I shall never understand the ways if your twisted civilization. I simply defend my honor and am condemned to life confinement, by a pig who sits on his royal ass wooing whores, and knows nothing of the affairs of the land he imagines to rule!" Lectures Grignr ?

"Enough of this! Away with the slut before I loose my control!"

Seeing the peril of his position, Grignr searched for an opening. Crushing prudence to the sward, he plowed into the soldier at his left arm taking hold of his sword, and bounding to the dias supporting the prince before the startled guards could regain their composure.

Agafnd leaped Grignr and his sire, but found a sword blade permeating the length of his ribs before he could loosed his weapon.

The councilor slumped to his knees as Grignr slid his crimsoned blade from Agfnd's rib cage. The fat prince stood undulating in insurmountable fear before the edge of the fiery maned comet, his flabs of jellied blubber pulsating to and fro in ripples of flowing terror.

"Where is your wisdom and power now, your magjesty?" Growled Grignr.

The prince went rigid as Grignr discerned him glazing over his shoulder. He swlived to note the cause of the noble's attention, raised his sword over his head, and prepared to leash a vicious downward cleft, but fell short as the haft of a steel rimed pike clashed against his unguarded skull. Then blackness and solitude. Silence enshrouding and ever peaceful reind supreme.

"Before me, sirrah! Before me as always! Ha, Ha Ha, Haaaa...", nobly cackled.

THree

Consciousness returned to Grignr in stygmatic pools as his mind gradually cleared of the cobwebs cluttering its inner recesses, yet the stygian cloud of charcoal ebony remained. An incompatible shield of blackness, enhanced by the bleak abscense of sound.

Grignr's muddled brain reeled from the shock of the blow he had recieved to the base of his skull. The events leading to his predicament were slow to filter back to him. He dickered with the notion that he was dead and had descended or sunk, however it may be, to the shadowed land beyond the the aperature of the grave, but rejected this hypothesis when his memory sifted back within his grips. This was not the land of the dead, it was something infinitely more precarious than anything the grave could offer. Death promised an infinity of peace, not the finite misery of an inactive life of confined torture, forever concealed from the life bearing shafts of the beloved rising sun. The orb that had been before taken for granted, yet now cherished above all else. To be forever refused further glimpses of the snow capped summits of the land of his birth, never again to witness the thrill of plundering unexplored lands beyond the crest of a bleeding horizon, and perhaps worst of all the denial to ever again encompass the lustful excitement of caressing the naked curves of the body of a trim yound wench.

This was indeed one of the buried chasms of Hell concealed within the inner depths of the palace's despised interior. A fearful ebony chamber devised to drive to the brinks of insanity the minds of the unfortunately condemned, through the inapt solitude of a limbo of listless dreary silence.

THree-anD-a-HaLF

A tightly rung elliptical circle or torches cast their wavering shafts prancing morbidly over the smooth surface of a rectangular, ridged alter. Expertly chisled forms of grotesque gargoyles graced the oblique rim protruberating the length of the grim orifice of death, staring forever ahead into nothingness in complete ignorance of the bloody rites enacted in their prescence. Brown flaking stains decorated the golden surface of the ridge surrounding the alter, which banked to a small slit at the lower right hand corner of the altar. The slit stood above a crudely pounded pail which had several silver meshed chalices hanging at its sides. Dangling at the rimof golden mallet, the handle of which was engraved with images of twisted faces and groved at its far end with slots designed for a snug hand grip. The head of the mallet was slightly larger than a clenched fist and shaped into a smooth oval mass.

Encircling the marble altar was a congregation of leering shamen. Eerie chants of a bygone age, originating unknown eons before the memory of man, were being uttered from the buried recesses of the acolytes' deep lings. Orange paint was smeared in generous globules over the tops of thw Priests' wrinkled shaven scalps, while golden rings projected from the lobes of their pink ears. Ornate robes of lusciour purple satin enclosed their bulging torsos, attached around their waists with silvered silk lashes latched with ebony buckles in the shape of morose mis-shaped skulls. Dangling around their necks were oval fashoned medalions held by thin gold chains, featuring in their centers blood red rubys which resembled crimson fetish eyeballs. Cushoning their bare feet were plush red felt slippers with pointed golden spikes projecting from their tips.

Situated in front of the altar, and directly adjacent to the copper pail was a massive jade idol; a misshaped, hideous bust of the shamens' pagan diety. The shimmering green idol was placed in a sitting posture on an ornately carved golden throne raised upon a round, dvory plated dias; it bulging arms and webbed hands resting on the padded arms of the seat. Its head was entwined in golden snake-like coils hanging over its oblong ears, which tappered off to thin hollow points. Its nose was a bulging triangular mass, sunken in at its sides with tow gaping nostrils. Dramatic beneath the nostrils was a twisted, shaggy lipped mouth, giving the impression of a slovering sadistic grimace.

At the foot of the heathen diety a slender, pale faced female, naked but for a golden, jeweled harness enshrouding her huge outcropping breasts, supporting long silver laces which extended to her thigh, stood before the pearl white field with noticable shivers traveling up and down the length of her exquisitely molded body. Her delicate lips trembled beneath soft narrow hands as she attemped to conceal herself from the piercing stare of the ambivalent idol.

Glaring directly down towards her was the stoney, cycloptic face of the bloated diety. Gaping from its single obling socket was scintillating, many fauceted scarlet emerald, a brilliant gem seeming to possess a life all of its own. A priceless gleaming stone, capable of domineering the wealth of conquering empires...the eye of Argon.

Four

All knowledge of measuring time had escaped Grignr. When a person is deprived of the sun, moon, and stars, he looses all conception of time as he had previously understood it. It seemed as if years had passed if time were being measured by terms of misery and mental anguish, yet he estimated that his stay had only been a few days in length. He has slept three times and had been fed five times since his awakening in the crypt. However, when the actions of the body are restricted its needs are also affected. The need for nourishmnet and slumber are directly proportional to the functions the body has performed, meaning that when free and active Grignr may become hungry every six hours and witness the desire for sleep every fifteen hours, whereas in his present condition he may encounter the need for food every ten hours, and the want for rest every twenty hours. All methods he had before depended upon were extinct in the dismal pit. Hence, he may have been imprisoned for ten minutes or ten years, he did not know, resulting in a disheartened emotion deep within his being.

The food, if you can honor the moldering lumps of fetid mush to that extent, was born to him by two guards who opened a portal at the top of his enclosure and shoved it to him in wooden bowls, retrieving the food and water bowels from his previous meal at the same time, after which they threw back the bolts on the iron latch and returned to their other duties. Since deprived of all other means of nourishment, Grignr was impelled to eat the tainted slop in order to ward off the paings of starvation, though as he stuffed it into his mouth with his filthy fingers and struggled to force it down his throat, he imagined it was that which had been spurned by the hounds stationed at various segments of the palace.

There was little in the baren vault that could occupy his body or mind. He had paced out the length and width of the enclosure time and time again and tested every granite slab which consisted the walls of the prison in hopes of finding a hidden passage to freedom, all of which was to no avail other than to keep him busy and distract his mind from wandering to thoughts of what he believed was his future. He had memorized the number of strides from one end to the other of the cell, and knew the exact number of slabs which made up the bleak dungeon. Numorous schemes were introduced and alternately discarded in turn as they succored to unravel to him no means of escape which stood the slightest chance of sucess.

Anguish continued to mount as his means of occupation were rapidly exhausted. Suddenly without no tive, he wasrouted from his contemplations as he detected a faint scratching sound at the end of the crypt opposite him. The sound seemed to be caused by something trying to scrape away at the grantite blocks the floor of the enclosure consisted of, the sandy scratching of something like an animal's claws.

Grignr gradually groped his way to the other end of the vault carefully feeling his way along with his hands ahead of him. When a few inches from the wall, a loud, penetrating squeal, and the scampering of small padded feet reverberated from the walls of the roughly hewn chamber.

Grignr threw his hands up to shield his face, and flung himself backwards upon his buttocks. A fuzzy form bounded to his hairy chest, burying its talons in his flesh while gnashing toward his throat with its grinding white teeth;its sour, fetid breath scortching the sqirming barbarians dilating nostrils. Grignr grappled with the lashing flexor muscles of the repugnant body of a garganuan brownhided rat, striving to hold its razor teeth from his juicy jugular, as its beady grey organs of sight glazed into the flaring emeralds of its prey.

Taking hold of the rodent around its lean, growling stomach with both hands Grignr pried it from his crimson rent breast, removing small patches of flayed flesh from his chest in the motion between the squalid black claws of the starving beast. Holding the rodent at arms length, he cupped his righthand over its frothing face, contrcting his fingers into a vice-like fist over the quivering head. Retaining his grips on the rat, grignr flexed his outstretched arms while slowly twisting his right hand clockwise and his left hand counter clockwise motion. The rodent let out a tortured squall, drawing scarlet as it violently dug its foam flecked fangs into the barbarians sweating palm, causing his face to contort to an ugly grimace as he cursed beneath his braeth.

With a loud crack the rodents head parted from its squirming torso, sending out a sprinking shower of crimson gore, and trailing a slimy string of disjointed vertebrae, snapped trachea, esophagus, and jugular, disjointed hyoid bone, morose purpled stretched hide, and blood seared muscles.

Flinging the broken body to the floor, Grignr shook his blood streaked hands and wiped them against his thigh until dry, then wiped the blood that had showered his face and from his eyes. Again sitting himself upon the jagged floor, he prepared to once more revamp his glum meditations. He told himself that as long as he still breathed the gust of life through his lungs, hope was not lost; he told himself this, but found it hard to comprehend in his gloomy surroundings. Yet he was still alive, his bulging sinews at their peak of marvel, his struggling mind floating in a miral of impressed excellence of thought. Plot after plot sifted through his mind in energetic contemplations.

Then it hit him. Minutes may have passed in silent thought or days, he could not tell, but he stumbled at last upon a plan that he considered as holding a slight margin of plausibility.

He might die in the attempt, but he knew he would not submit without a final bloody struggle. It was not a foolproof plan, yet it built up a store of renewed vortexed energy in his overwroughtsoul, though he might perish in the execution of the escape, he would still be escaping the life of infinite torture in store forhim. Either way he would still cheat the gloating prince of the succored revenge his sadistic mind craved so dearly.

The guards would soon come to bear him off to the prince's buried mines of dread, giving him the sought after opportunity to execute his newly formulated plan. Groping his way along the rough floor Grignr finally found his tool in a pool of congealed gore; the carcass of the decapitated rodent; the tool that the very filth he had been sentenced too, spawned. When the time came for action he would have to be prepared, so he set himself to rending the sticky hulk in grim silence, searching by the touch of his fingertips for the lever to freedom.

Five

"Up to the altar and be done with it wench;" ordered a fidgeting shaman as he gave the female a grim stare accompanied by the wrinkling of his lips to a mirthful grin of delight.

The girl burst into a slow steady whimper, stooping shakily to her knees and cringing woefully from the priest with both arms wound snake-like around the bulging jade jade shin rising before her scantily attired figure. Her face was redly inflamed from the salty flow of tears spouting from her glassy dilated eyeballs.

With short, heavy footfals the priest approached the female, his piercing stare never wavering from her quivering young countenance. Halting before the terrified girl he projected his arm outward and motioned her to arise with an upward movement of his hand. the girl's whimpering increased slightly and she sunk closer to the floor rather than arising. The flickering torches outlined her trim build with a weird ornate glow as it cast a ghostly shadow dancing in horrid waves of splendor over smoothly worn whiteness of the marble hewn altar.

The shaman's lips curled back farther, exposing a set of blackened, decaying molars which transformed his slovenly grin into a wide greasy arc of sadistic mirth and alternately interposed into the female a strong sensation of stomach curdling nausea. "Have it as you will female;" gloated the enhanced priest as he bent over at the waist, projecting his ape-like arms forward, and clasped the female's slender arms with his hairy round fists. With an inward surge of of his biceps he harshly jerked the trembling girl to her feet and smothered her salty wet cheeks with the moldy touch of his decrepid, dull red lips.

The vile stench of the Shaman's hot fetid breath over came the nauseated female with a deep soul searing sickness, causing her to wrench her head backwards and regurgitate a slimy, orangewhite stream of swelling gore over the richly woven purple robe of the enthused acolyte.

The priest's lips trembled with a malicious rage as he removed his callous paws from the girl's arms and replaced them with tightly around her undulating neck, shaking her violently to and fro.

The girl gasped a tortured groan from her clamped lungs, her sea blue eyes bulging forth from damp sockets. Cocking her right foot backwards, she leashed it desperately outwards with the strength of a demon possessed, lodging her sandled foot squarely between the shaman's testicles.

The startled priest released his crushing grip, crimping his body over at the waist overlooking his recessed belly; wide open in a deep chasim. His face flushed to a rose red shade of crimson, eyelids fluttering wide with eyeballs protruding blindly outwards from their sockets to their outmost perimeters, while his lips quivered wildly about allowing an agonized wallow to gust forth as his breath billowed from burning lungs. His hands reached out clutching his urinary gland as his knees wobbled rapidly about for a few seconds then buckled, causing the ruptured shaman to collapse in an egg huddled mass to the granite pavement, rolling helplessly about in his agony.

The pathetic screeches of the shaman groveling in dejected misery upon the hand hewn granite laid pavement, worn smooth by countless hours of arduous sweat and toil, a welter of ichor oozing through his clenched hands, attracted the purturbed attention of his comrades from their foetid ulations. The actions of this this rebellious wench bespoke the creedence of an unheard of sacrilige. Never before in a lost maze of untold eons had a chosen one dared to demonstrate such blasphemy in the face of the cult's idolic diety.

The girl cowered in unreasoning terror, helpless in the face of the emblazoned acolytes' rage; her orchid tusseled face smothered betwixt her bulging bosom as she shut her curled lashed tightly hoping to open them and find herself awakening from a morbid nightmare. yet the hand of destiny decreed her no such mercy, the antagonized pack of leering shaman converging tensely upon her prostrate form were entangled all too lividly in the grim web of reality.

Shuddering from the clamy touch of the shaman as they grappled with her supple form, hands wrenching at her slender arms and legs in all directions, her bare body being molested in the midst of a labyrnth of orange smudges, purpled satin, and mangled skulls, shadowed in an eerie crimson glow; her confused head reeled then clouded in a mist of enshrouding ebony as she lapsed beneath the protective sheet of unconsiousness to a land peach and resign.

SIX

"Take hold of this rope," said the first soldier, "and climb out from your pit, slut. Your presence is requested in another far deeper hell hole."

Grignr slipped his right hand to his thigh, concealing a small opaque object beneath the folds of the g-string wrapped about his waist. Brine wells swelled in Grignr's cold, jade squinting eyes, which grown accustomed to the gloom of the stygian pools of ebony engulfing him, were bedazzled and blinded by flickerering radiance cast forth by the second soldiers's resin torch.

Tightly gripped in the second soldier's right hand, opposite the intermittent torch, was a large double edged axe, a long leather wound oaken handled transfixing the center of the weapon's iron head. Adorning the torso's of both of the sentries were thin yet sturdy hauberks, the breatplates of which were woven of tightly hemmed twines of reinforced silver braiding. Cupping the soldiers' feet were thick leather sandals, wound about their shins to two inches below their knees. Wrapped about their waists were wide satin girdles, with slender bladed poniards dangling loosely from them, the hilts of which featured scarlet encrusted gems. Resting upon the manes of their heads, and reaching midway to their brows were smooth copper morions. Spiraling the lower portion of the helmet were short, up-curved silver spikes, while a golden hump spired from the top of each basinet. Beneath their chins, wound around their necks, and draping their clad shoulders dangled regal purple satin cloaks, which flowed midway to the soldiers feet.

hand over hand, feet braced against the dank walls of the enclosure, huge Grignr ascended from the moldering dephs of the forlorn abyss. His swelled limbs, stiff due to the boredom of a timeless inactivity, compounded by the musty atmosture and jagged granite protuberan against his body, craved for action. The opportunity now presenting itself served the purpose of oiling his rusty joints, and honing his dulled senses.

He braced himself, facing the second soldier. The sentry's stature was was wildly exaggerated in the glare of the flickering cresset cuppex in his right fist. His eyes were wide open in a slightly slanted

THE NEW NEW ULTRA WEIRD

owlish glaze, enhanced in their sinister intensity by the hawk-bill curve of his nose andpale yellow pique of his cheeks.

"Place your hands behind your back," said the second soldier as he raised his ax over his right shoulder blade and cast it a wavering glance. "We must bind your wrists to parry any attempts at escape. Be sure to make the knot a stout one, Broig, we wouldn't want our guest to take leave of our guidance."

Broig grasped Grignr's left wrist and reached for the barbarians's right wrist. Grignr wrenched his right arm free and swivleed to face Broig, reach- beneath his loin cloth with his right hand. The sentry grappled at his girdle for the sheathed dagger, but recoiled short of his intentions as Grignr's right arm swept to his gorge. The soldier went limp, his bobbing eyes rolling beneath fluttering eyelids, a deep welt across his spouting gullet. Without lingering to observe the result of his efforts, Grignr dropped to his knees. The second soldier's axe cleft over Grignr's head in a blze of silvered ferocity, severing several scarlet locks from his scalp. Coming to rest in his fellow's stomach, the iron head crashed through mail and flesh with splintering force, spilling a pool of crimsoned entrails over the granite paving.

Before the sentry could wrench his axe free from his comrade's carcass, he found Grignr's massive hands clasped about his throat, choking the life from his clamped lungs. With a zealous grunt, the Ecordian flexed his tightly corded biceps, forcing the grim faced soldier to one knee. The sentry plunged his right fist into Grignr's face, digging his grimy nails into the barbarians flesh. Ejaculating a curse through rasping teeth, grignr surged the bulk of his weight foreard, bowling the beseiged soldier over upon his back. The sentry's arms collapsed to his thigh, shuddering convulsively; his bulging eyes staring blindly from a bloated ,cherry red face.

Rising to his feet, Grignr shook the bllod from his eyes, ruffling his surly red mane as a brush fire swaying to the nightime breeze. Stooping over the spr sprawled corpse of the first soldier, Grignr retrieved a small white object from a pool of congealing gore. Snorting a gusty billow of mirth, he once more concealed th e tiny object beneath his loin cloth; the tediously honed pelvis bone of the broken rodent. Returning his attention toward the second soldier, Grignr turned to the task of attiring his limbs. To move about freely through the dim recesses of the castle would require the grotesque garb of its soldiery.

Utilizing the silence and stealth aquired in the untamed climbs of his childhood, Grignr slink through twisting corridors, and winding stairways, lighting his way with the confisticated torch of his dispatched guardian. Knowing where his steps were leading to, Grignr meandered aimlessly in search of an exit from the chateau's dim confines. The wild blood coarsing through his veins yearned for the undefiled freedom of the livid wilderness lands.

Coming upon a fork in the passage he treaked, voices accompanied by clinking footfalls discerned to his sensitive ears from the left corridor. Wishing to avoid contact, Grignr veered to the right passageway. If aquested as to the purpose of his presence, his barbarous accent would reveal his identity, being that his attire was not that of the castle's mercenary troops.

In grim silence Grignr treaded down the dingily lit corridor; a stalking panther creeping warily along on padded feet. After an interminable period of wandering through the dull corridors; no gaps to break the monotony of the cold gray walls, Grignr espied a small winding stairway. Descending the flight of arced granite slabs to their posterior, Grignr was confronted by a short haalway leading to a tall arched wooden doorway.

Halting before the teeming portal portal, Grignr restes his shaggy head sideways against the barrier. Detecting no sounds from within, he grasped the looped metel handle of the door; his arms surging with a tremendous effort of bulging muscles, yet the door would not budge. Retrieving his ax from where he had sheathed it beneath his girdle, he hefted it in his mighty hands with an apiesed grunt, and wedging one of its blackened edges into the crack between the portal and its iron rimed sill. Bracing his sandaled right foot against the rougjly hewn wall, teeth tightly clenched, Grignr appilevered the oaken haft, employing it as a lever whereby to pry open the barrier. The leather wound hilt bending to its utmost limits of endurance, the

THE NEW NEW ULTRA WEIRD

massive portal swung open with a grating of snapped latch and rusty iron hinges.

Glancing about the dust swirled room in the gloomily dancing glare of his flickering cresset, Grignr eyed evidences of the enclosure being nothing more than a forgotten storeroom. Miscellaneous articles required for the maintainance of a castle were piled in disorganized heaps at infrequent intervals toward the wall opposite the barbarian's piercing stare. Utilizing long, bounding strides, Grignr paced his way over to the mounds of supplies to discover if any articles of value were contained within their midst.

Detecting a faint clinking sound, Grignr sprawed to his left side with the speed of a striking cobra, landing harshly upon his back; torch and axe loudly clattering to the floor in a morass of sparks and flame. A elmwoven board leaped from collapsed flooring, clashing against the jagged flooring and spewing a shower of orange and yellow sparks over Grignr's startled face. Rising uneasily to his feet, the half stunned Ecordian glared down at the grusome arm of death he had unwittingly sprung. "Mrifk!"

If not for his keen auditory organs and lighting steeled reflexes, Grignr would have been groping through the shadowed hell-pits of the Grim Reaper. He had unknowingly stumbled upon an ancient, long forgotton booby trap; a mistake which would have stunted the perusal of longevity of one less agile. A mechanism, similar in type to that of a minature catapult was concealed beneath two collapsable sections of granite flooring. The arm of the device was four feet long, boasting razor like cleats at regular intervals along its face with which it was to skewer the luckless body of its would be victim. Grignr had stepped upon a concealed catch which relaesed a small metal latch beneath the two granite sections, causing them to fall inward, and thereby loose the spiked arm of death they precariously held in.

Partially out of curiosity and partially out of an inordinate fear of becoming a pincushion for a possible second trap, Grignr plunged his torch into the exposed gap in the floor. The floor of a second chamber stood out seven feet below the glare. Tossing his torch through the aperature, Grignr grasped the side of an adjoining tile, dropping down.

Glancing about the room, Grignr discovered that he had decended into the palace's mausoleum. Rectangular stone crypts cluttered the floor at evenly placed intervals. The tops of the enclosures were plated with thick layers of virgin gold, while the sides were plated with white ivory; at one time sparkling, but now grown dingy through the passage of the rays of allencompassing mother time. Featured at the head of each sarcophagus in tarnished silver was an expugnisively carved likeness of its rotting inhabitant.

A dingy atmosphere pervaded the air of the chamber; which sealed in the enclosure for an unknown period had grown thick and stale. Intermingling with the curdled currents was the repugnant stench of slowly moldering flesh, creeping ever slowly but surely through minute cracks in the numerous vaults. Due to the embalming of the bodies, their flesh decayed at a much slower rate than is normal, yet the nauseous oder was none the less repellant.

Towering over Grignr's head was the trap he released. The mechanism of the miniaturized catapolt was cluttered with mildew and cobwebs. Notwithstanding these relics of antiquity, its efficiency remained unimpinged. To the right of the trap wound a short stairway through a recess in the ceiling; a concealed entrance leading to the mausoleum for which the catapult had obviously been erected as a silent, relentless guardian.

Climbing up the side of the device, Grignr set to the task of resetting its mechanism. In the e event that a search was organized, it would prove well to leave no evidence of his presence open to wandering eyes. Besides, it might even serve to dwindle the size of an opposing force.

Descending from his perch, Grignr was startled by a faintly muffled scream of horrified desperation. His hair prickled yawkishly in disorganized clumps along his scalp. As a cold danced along the length of his spinal cord. No moral/mortal barrier, human or otherwise, was capable of arousing the numbing sensation of fear inside of Grignr's smoldering soul. However, he was overwrought by the forces of the barbarians' instinctive fear of the supernatural. His mighty thews had always served to adequately conquer any tangible foe., but the intangible was something distant and terrible. Dim horrifying tales passed by word of mouth over glimmering camp fires and skins of wine had more than once served the purpose of chilling the marrowed core of his sturdy limbed bones.

Yet, the scream contained a strangely human quality, unlike that which Grignr imagined would come from the lungs of a demon or spirit, making Grignr take short nervous strides advancing to the sarcophagus from which the sound was issuing. Clenching his teeth in an attempt to steel his jangled nerves, Grignr slid the engraved slab from the vault with a sharp rasp of grinding stone. Another long drawn cry of terror infested anguish met the barbarian, scoring like the shrill piping of a demented banshee; piercing the inner fibres of his superstitious brain with primitive dread dread and awe.

Stooping over to espy the tomb's contents, the glittering Ecordians nostrills were singed by the scorching aroma of a moldering corpse, long shut up and fermenting; the same putrid scent which permeated the entire chamber, though multiplied to a much more concentrated dosage. The shriveled, leathery packet of crumbling bones and dried flacking flesh offered no resistance, but remained in a fixed position of perpetual vigilance, watching over its dim abode from hollow gaping sockets.

The tortured crys were not coming from the tomb but from some hidden depth below! Pulling the reaking corpse from its resting place, Grignr tossed it to the floor in a broken, mangled heap. Upon one side of the crypt's bottom was attached a series of tiny hinges while running parallel along the opposite side of a convex railing like protruberance; laid so as to appear as a part of the interior surface of the sarcophagus.

Raising the slab upon its bronze hinges, long removed from the gaze of human eyes, Grignr percieved a scene which caused his blood to smolder not unlike bubbling, molten lava. Directly below him a whimpering female lay stretched upon a smooth surfaced marble altar. A pack of grasy faced shamen clustered around her in a tight circular formation. Crouched over the girl was a tall, potbellied priest; his face dominated by a disgusting, open mouthed grimace of sadistic glee. Suspended from the acolyte's clenched right hand was a carven oval faced mallet, which he waved menacingly over the girl's shadowed face; an incoherent gibberish flowing from his grinning, thick lipped mouth.

In the face of the amorphos, broad breated female, stretched out aluringly before his gaping eyes; the universal whim of nature filing a plea of despair inside of his white hot soul; Grignr acted in the only manner he could perceive. Giving vent to a hoarse, throat rending battle cry, Grignr plunged into the midst of the startled shamen; torch simmering in his left hand andax twirling in his right hand.

A gaunt skull faced priest standing at the far side of the altar clutched desperately at his throat, coughing furiously in an attempt to catch his breath. Lurching helplessly to and fro, the acolyte pitched headlong against the gleaming base of a massive jade idol. Writhing agonizedly against the hideous image, foam flecking his chalk white lips, the priest struggled helplessly - - - the victim of an epileptic siezure.

Startled by the barbarians stunning appearance, the chronic fit of their fellow, and the fear that Grignr might be the avantgarde of a conquering force dedicated to the cause of destroying their degenerated cult, the saman momentarily lost their composure. Giving vent to heedless pandemonium, the priests fell easy prey to Grignr's sweeping arc of crimsoned death and maiming distruction.

The acolyte performing the sacrifice took a vicious blow to the stomach; hands clutching vitals and severed spinal cord as he sprawled over the altar. The disor anized priests lurched and staggered with split skulls, dismembered limbs, and spewing entrails before the enraged Ecordian's relentless onslaught. The howles of the maimed and dying reverberated against the walls of the tiny chamber; a chorus of hell frought despair; as the granite floor ran red with blood. The entire chamber was encompassed in the heat of raw savage butchery as Grignr luxuriated in the grips of a primitive, beastly blood lust.

Presently all went silenet save for the ebbing groans of the sinking shaman and Grignr's heaving breath accompanied by several gusty curses. The well had run dry. No more lambs remained for the slaughter.

The rampaging stead of death having taken of Grignr for the moment, left the barbarian free to the exploitation of his other perusials. Towering over his head was the misshaped image of the cult's hideous diety - - - Argon. The fantastic size of the idol in consideration of its being of pure jade was enough to cause the senses of any man to stagger and reel, yet thus was not the case for the behemoth. he had paid only casual notice to this incredible fact, while riviting the whole of his attention upon the jewel protruding from the idol's sole socket; its masterfully cut faucets emitting blinding rays of hypnotising beauty. After all, a man cannot slink from a heavily guarded palace while burdened down by the intense bulk of a squatting statue, providing of course that the idol can even be hefted, which in fact was beyond the reaches of Grignr's coarsing stamina. On the other hand, the jewel, gigantic as it was, would not present a hinderence of any mean concern.

"Help me ... please ... I can make it well worth your while," pleaded a soft, anguish strewn voice wafting over Grignr's shoulders as he plucked the dull red emerald from its roots. Turning, Grignr faced the female that had lured him into this blood bath, but whom had become all but forgotten in the heat of the battle.

"You"; ejaculated the Ecordian in a pleased tone. "I though that I had seen the last of you at the tavern, but verilly I was mistaken." Grignr advanced into the grips of the female's entrancing stare, severing the golden chains that held her captive upon the altars highly polished face of ornamental limestone.

As Grignr lifted the girl from the altar, her arms wound dexterously about his neck; soft and smooth against his harsh exterior. "Art thou pleased that we have chanced to meet once again?" Grignr merely voiced an sighed grunt, returning the damsels embrace while he smothered her trim, delicate lips between the coarsing protrusions of his reeking maw.

"Let us take leave of this retched chamber." Stated Grignr as he placed the female upon her feet. She swooned a moment, causing Grignr to giver her support then regained her stance. "Art thou able to find your way through the accursed passages of this castle? Mrifk! Every one of the corridors of this damned place are identical."

"Aye; I was at one time a slave of prince Agaphim. His clammy touch sent a sour swill through my belly, but my efforts reaped a harvest. I gained the pig's liking whereby he allowed me the freedom of the palace. It was through this means that I eventually managed escape at the western gate. His trust found him with a dagger thrust his ribs," the wench stated whimsicoracally.

"What were you doing at the tavern whence I discovered you?" asked Grignr as he lifted the female through the opening into the mausoleum.

"I had sought to lay low from the palace's guards as they conducted their search for me. The tavern was seldom frequented by the palace guards and my identity was unknown to the common soldiers. It was through the disturbance that you caused that the palace guards were attracted to the tavern. I was dragged away shortly after you were escorted to the palace."

"What are you called by female?"

"Carthena, daughter of Minkardos, Duke of Barwego, whose lands border along the northwestern fringes of Gorzom. I was paid as homage to Agaphim upon his thirty-eighth year," husked the femme!

"And I am called a barbarian!" Grunted Grignr in a disgusted tone!

"Aye! The ways of our civilization are in many ways warped and distorted, but what is your calling," she queried, bustily?

"Grignr of Ecordia."

"Ah, I have heard vaguely of Ecordia. It is the hill country to the far east of the Noregolean Empire. I have also heard Agaphim curse your land more than once when his troops were routed in the unaccustomed mountains and gorges." Sayeth she.

"Aye. My people are not tarnished by petty luxuries and baubles. They remain fierce and unconquerable in their native climes." After reaching the hidden panel at the head of the stairway, Grignr was at a loss in regard to its operation. His fiercest heaves were as pebbles against burnished armour! Carthena depressed a small symbol included within the elaborate design upon the panel whereopen it slowly slid into a cleft in the wall. "How did you come to be the victim of those crazed shamen?" Quested Grignr as he escorted Carthena through the piles of rummage on the left side of the trap.

"By Agaphim's orders I was thrust into a secluded cell to await his passing of sentence. By some means, the Priests of Argon acquired a set of keys to the cell. They slew the guard placed over me and abducted me to the chamber in which you chanced to come upon the scozsctic sacrifice. Their hell-spawned cult demands a sacrifice once every three moons upon its full journey through the heavens. They were startled by your unannounced appearance through the fear that you had been sent by Agaphim. The prince would surely have submitted them to the most ghastly of tortures if he had ever discovered their unfaithfulness to Sargon, his bastard diety. Many of the partakers of the ritual were high nobles and high trustees of the inner palace; Agaphim's pittiless wrath would have been unparalled."

"They have no more to fear of Agaphim now!" Bellowed Grignr in a deep mirthful tome; a gleeful smirk upon his face. "I have seen that they were delivered from his vengence."

Engrossed by Carthena's graceful stride and conversation Grignr failed to take note of the footfalls rapidly approaching behind him. As he swung aside the arched portal linking the chamber with the corridors beyond, a maddened, blood lusting screech reverberated from his ear drums. Seemingly utilizing the speed of thought, Grignr swiveled to face his unknown foe. With gaping eyes and widened jaws, Grignr raised his axe above his surly mein; but he was too late.

seven

With wobbling knees and swimming head, the priest that had lapsed into an epileptic siezure rose unsteadily to his feet. While enacting his choking fit in writhing agony, the shaman was overlooked by Grignr. The barbarian had mistaken the siezure for the death throes of the acolyte, allowing the priest to avoid his stinging blade. The sight that met the priests inflamed eyes nearly served to sprawl him upon the floor once more. The sacrificial sat it grim, blood splattered silence all around him, broken only by the occasional yelps and howles of his maimed and butchered fellows. Above his head rose the hideous idol, its empty socket holding the shaman's ifurbished infuriated gaze.

His eyes turned to a stoney glaze with the realization of the pillage and blasphemy. Due to his high succeptibility following the siezure, the priest was transformed into a raving maniac bent soley upon reaking vengeance. With lips curled and quivering, a crust of foam dripping from them, the acolyte drew a long, wicked looking jewel hilted scimitar from his silver girdle and fled through the aperature in the ceiling uttering a faintly perceptible ceremonial jibberish.

seven-and-a-Half

A sweeping scimitar swung towards Grignr's head in a shadowed blur of motion. With Axe raised over his head, Grignr prepared to parry the blow, while gaping wideeyed in open mouthed perplexity. Suddenly a sharp snap resounded behind the frothing shaman. The scimitar, halfway through its fatal sweep, dropped from a quivering nerveless hand, clattering harmlessly to the stoneage. Cutting his screech short with a bubbling, red mouthed gurgle, the lacerated acolyte staggered under the pressure of the released spring-board. After a moment of hopeless struggling, the shaman buckled, sprawling face down in a widening pool of bllod and entrails, his regal purple robe blending enhancingly with the swirling streams of crimson.

"Mrifk! I thought I had killed the last of those dogs;" muttered Grignr in a half apathetic state.

"Nay Grignr. You doubtless grew careless while giving vent to your lusts. But let us not tarry any long lest we over tax the fates. The paths leading to freedom will soon be barred.

The wretch's crys must certainly have attracted unwanted attention," the wench mused.

"By what direction shall we pursue our flight?"

"Up that stair and down the corridor a short distance is the concealed enterance to a tunnel seldom used by others than the prince, and known to few others save the palace's royalty. It is used mainly by the prince when he wishes to take leave of the palace in secret. It is not always in the Prince's best interests to leave his chateau in public view. Even while under heavy guard he is often assaulted by hurtling stones and rotting fruits. The commoners have little love for him." lectured the nerelady!

"It is amazing that they would ever have left a pig like him become their ruler. I should imagine that his people would rise up and crucify him like the dog he is."

"Alas, Grignr, it is not as simple as all that. His soldiers are well paid by him. So long as he keeps their wages up they will carry out his damned wished. The crude impliments of the commonfolk would never stand up under an onslaught of forged blades and protective armor; they would be going to their own slaughter," stated Carthena to a confused, but angered Grignr as they topped the stairway.

"Yet how can they bear to live under such oppression? I would sooner die beneath the sword than live under such a dog's command." added Grignr as the pair stalked down the hall in the direction opposite that in which Grignr had come.

"But all men are not of the same mold that you are born of, they choose to live as they are so as to save their filthy necks from the chopping block." Returned Carthena in a disgusted tone as she cast an appiesed glance towards the stalwart figure at her side whose left arm was wound dextrously about her slim waist; his slowly waning torch casting their images in intermingling wisps as it dangled from his left hand.

Presently Carthena came upon the panel, concealed amonst the other granite slabs and discernable only by the burned out cresset above it. "As I push the cresset aside push the panel inwards." Catrhena motioned to the panel she was refering to and twisted the cresset in a counterclockwise motion. Grignr braced his right shoulder against the walling, concentrating the force of his bulk against it. The slab gradually swung inward with a slight grating sound. Carthena stooped beneath Grignr's corded arms and crawled upon all fours into the passage beyond. Grignr followed after easing the slab back into place.

Winding before the pair was a dark musty tunnel, exhibiting tangled spider webs from it ceiling to wall and an oozing, sickly slime running lazily upon its floor. Hanging from the chipped wall upon GrignR's right side was a half mouldered corpse, its grey flacking arms held in place by rusted iron manacles. Carthena flinched back into Grignr's arms at sight of the leering set in an ugly distorted grimmace; staring horribly at her from hollow gaping sockets.

"This alcove must also be used by Agaphim as a torture chamber. I wonder how many of his enemies have disappeared into these haunts never to be heard from again," pondered the hulking brute.

"Let us flee before we are also caught within Agaphim's ghastly clutches. The exit from this tunnel cannot be very far from here!" Said Carthena with a slight sob to her voice, as she sagged in Grignr's encompasing embrace.

"Aye; It will be best to be finished with this corridor as soon as it is possible. But why do you flinch from the sight of death so? Mrift! You have seen much death this day without exhibiting such emotions." Exclaimed Grignr as he led her trembling form along the dingy confines.

"---The man hanging from the wall was Doyanta. He had committed the folly of showing affections for me in front of Agaphim --- he never meant any harm by his actions!" At this Carthena broke into a slow steady whimpering, chokking her voice with gasping sobs. "There was never anything between us yet Agaphim did this to him! The beast! May the demons of Hell's deepest haunts claw away at his wretched flesh for this merciless act!" she prayed.

"I detect that you felt more for this fellow than you wish to let on … but enough of this, We can talk of such matters after we are once more free to do so." With this Grignr lifted the grieved female to her feet and strode onward down the corridor, supporting the bulk of her weight with his surging left arm.

Presently a dim light was perceptibly filtering into the tunnel, casting a dim reddish hue upon the moldy wall of the passage's grim confines. Carthena had ceased her whimpering and partially regained her composure. "The tunnel's end must be nearing. Rays of sunlight are beginning to seep into …"

Grignr clameed his right hand over Carthena's mouth and with a slight struggle pulled her over to the shadows at the right hand wall of the path, while at the same time thrusting this torch beneath an overhanging stone to smother its flickering rays. "Be silent; I can hear footfalls approaching through the tunnel;" growled Grignr in a hushed tone.

"All that you hear are the horses corraled at the far end of the tunnel. That is a further sign that we are nearing our goal." She stated!

"All that you hear is less than I hear! I heard footsteps coming towards us. Silence yourself that we may find out whom we are being brought into contact with. I doubt that any would have thought as yet of searching this passage for us. The advantage of surprize will be upon our side." Grignr warned.

Carthena cast her eyes downward and ceased any further pursuit towards conversation, an irritating habit in which she had gained an amazing proficiency. Two figures came into the pairs view, from around a turn in the tunnel. They were clothed in rich luxuriant silks and rambling o on in conversation while ignorant of their crouching foes waiting in an ambush ahead.

"...That barbarian dog is cringing beneath the weight of the lash at this moment sire. He shall cause no more disturbance."

"Aye, and so it is with any who dare to cross the path of Sargon's chosen one." said the 2nd man.

"But the peasants are showing signs of growing unrest. They complain that they cannot feet their families while burdened with your taxes."

"I shall teach those sluts the meaning of humility! Order an immediate increase upon their taxes. They dare to question my sovereign authority, Ha-a, they shall soon learn what true oppression can be. I will ... "

A shodowed bulk leapt from behind a jutting promontory as it brought down a double edged axe with the spped of a striking thought. One of the nobles sagged lifeless to the ground, skull split to the teeth.

Grignr gasped as he observed the bisected face set in its leering death agonies. It was Agafnd! The dead mans comrade having recovered from his shock drew a jewel encrusted dagger from beneath the folds of his robe and lunged toward the barbarians back. Grignr spun at the sound from behind and smashed down his crimsoned axe once more. His antagonist lunged howling to a stream of stagnent green water, grasping a spouting stump that had once been a wrist. Grignr raised his axe over his head and prepared to finish the incomplete job, but was detered half way through his lunge by a frenzied screech from behind.

Carthena leapt to the head of the writhing figure, plunging a smoldering torch into the agonized face. The howls increased in their horrid intensity, stifled by the sizzling of roasting flesh, then died down until the man was reduced to a blubbering mass of squirming, insensate flesh.

Grignr advance to Carthena's side wincing slightly from the putrid aroma of charred flesh that rose in a puff of thick white smog throughout the chamber. Carthena reeled slightly, staring dasedly downward at her gruesome handywork. "I had to do it ... it was Agaphim ... I had to, " she exclaimed!

"Sargon should be more carful of his right hand men." Added Grignr, a smug grin upon his lips. "But to hell with Sargon for now, the stench is becoming bothersome to me." With that Grignr grasped Carthena around the waist leading her around the bend in the cave and into the open.

A ball of feral red was rising through the mists of the eastern horizon, disipating the slinking shadows of the night. A coral stood before the pair, enclosing two grazing mares. Grignr reached into a weighted down leather pouch dangling at his side and drew forth the scintillant red emerald he had obtained from the bloated idol. Raising it toward the sun he said, "We shall do well with bauble, eh!"

Carthena gaped at the gem gasping in a terrified manner "The eye of Argon, Oh! Kalla!" At this the gem gave off a blinding glow, then dribbled through Grignr's fingers in a slimy red ooze. Grignr stepped back, pushing Carthena behind him. The droplets of slime slowly converged into a pulsating jelly-like mass. A single opening transfixed the blob, forminf into a leechlike maw.

Then the hideous transgressor of nature flowed towards Grignr, a trail of greenish slime lingering behind it. The single gap puckered repeatedly emitting a ghastly sucking sound.

Grignr spread his legs into a battle stance, steeling his quivering thews for a battle royal with a thing he knew not how to fight. Carthena wound her arms about her protectors neck, mumbling, "Kill it! Kill!" While her entire body trembled.

The thing was almost upon Grignr when he buried his axe into the gristly maw. It passed through the blob and clanged upon the ground. Grignr drew his axe back with a film of yellow-green slime clinging to the blade. The thing was seemingly unaffected. Then it started to slooze up his leg. The hairs upon his nape stoode on end from the slimey feel of the things buly, bulk. The Nautous sucking sound became louder, and Grignr felt the blood being drawn from his body. With each hiss of hideous pucker the thing increased in size.

Grignr shook his foot about madly in an attempt to dislodge the blob, but it clung like a leech, still feeding upon his rapidly draining life fluid. He grasped with his hands trying to rip it off, but only found his hands entangled in a sickly gluelike substance. The slimey thing continued its puckering ; now having grown the size of Grignr's leg from its vampiric feast.

Grignr began to reel and stagger under the blob, his chalk white face and faltering muscles attesting to the gigantic loss of blood. Carthena slipped from Grignr in a death-like faint, a morrow chilling scream upon her red rubish lips. In final desperation Grignr grasped the smoldering torch upon the ground and plunged it into the reeking maw of the travestry. A shudder passed through the thing. Grignr felt the blackness closing upon his eyes, but held on with the last ebb of his rapidly waning vitality. He could feel its grip lessoning as a hideous gurgling sound erupted from the writhing maw. The jelly like mass began to bubble like a vat of boiling tar as quavers passed up and down its entire form.

With a sloshing plop the thing fell to the ground, evaporating in a thick scarlet cloud until it reatained its original size. It remained thus for a moment as the puckered maw took the shape of a protruding red eyeball, the pupil of which seemed to unravel before it the tale of creation. How a shapeless mass slithered from the quagmires of the stygmatic pool of time, only to degenerate into a leprosy of avaricious lust. In that fleeting moment the grim mystery of life was revealed before Grignr's ensnared gaze.

The eyeballs glare turned to a sudden plea of mercy, a plea for the whole of humanity. Then the blob began to quiver with violent convulsions; the eyeball shattered into a thousand tiny fragments and evaporated in a curling wisp of scarlet mist. The very ground below the thing began to vibrate and swallow it up with a belch.

The thing was gone forever. All that remained was a dark red blotch upon the face of the earth, blotching things up. Shaking his head, his shaggy mane to clear the jumbled fragments of his mind, Grignr tossed the limp female over his shoulder. Mounting one of the disgruntled mares, and leading the other; the weary, scarred barbarian trooted slowly off into the horizon to become a tiny pinpoint in a filtered filed of swirling blue mists, leaving the Nobles, soldiers and peasants to replace the missing monarch. Long leave the king!!!

CONFRONTATION—FROM AWOKEN

SERRA ELINSEN

Serra Elinsen in her own words is a part-time author, fulltime mother. The following story is an excerpt from her debut novel Awoken, *about a teenage girl who falls in love with Cthulhu. We found it to be exemplary of the New New Ultra Weird's flexibility with crossing over of genres.*

Though I barely slept at all, I spent the rest of the weekend in bed. I saw no point in getting up. I knew I wouldn't be able to focus on anything but my own thoughts, and I could just as easily do that lying down.

My mom came barging in every couple of hours, asking questions and looking at me as though I were dying. I must have said, "I'm fine, Mom," a dozen times. Of course, I wasn't fine, but she didn't need to know that. There was nothing she could have done to help me, except leave me alone with my thoughts. Again and again, I went over the events of the past week, trying to make sense of it all, but it was like trying to solve a jigsaw puzzle without all the pieces.

Riley had made Travis lose his mind. I was sure of it.

But how? And, more importantly, why?

I thought about Thursday in the parking lot at Henrietta's, when he'd vanished into thin air. The way he talked, like he was from another era. The fact that he'd appeared in my dreams before I'd met him in real life. The conclusion was as obvious as it was terrifying.

Riley Bay wasn't human.

But if he wasn't human, then what was he? An alien, sent to Earth to learn about humanity in preparation for an invasion? Riley was certainly weird enough to be an alien, but I didn't see why the mother ship would send him to Portsmouth, Rhode Island, in the guise of a high schooler. Surely, he would learn more by infiltrating our government or something, right?

If he wasn't from outer space, then he had to be from Earth. But if any native of Earth could do the things he did, then the world was a much stranger place than I'd been led to believe.

In my head, I made a list of every mythical beast I could think of, but Riley Bay didn't resemble any of them. He went out during the day, so he couldn't be a vampire. He was in school during the full moon, so he wasn't a werewolf. He didn't have wings, so I could cross both faery and angel off the list. What did that leave? Leprechauns? I snorted at the very idea.

And what was his motive? What interest could such a creature have in me, the most ordinary girl in the world? Why did he despise me so? And why punish Travis for taunting me? If anything, he should have reveled in seeing me humiliated like that. The more I learned about Riley Bay, the less he made sense.

A big part of me wanted to pretend the whole thing had never happened, but that was impossible. Even if my mind had let me forget, my classmates wouldn't have. On Monday, everyone was talking about Travis's unexpected mental break.

"They're saying it was drugs," Vik informed us at lunch.

"He didn't seem high to me," said Bree. "I mean, until he started screaming about tentacles."

"I guess whatever he took needed time to kick in," said Vik, shrugging.

"What did he take?" Bree asked. "LSD? Bath salts? Mushrooms?"

"I've heard conflicting things," said Vik. "But whatever it was, he must have way overdone it. They're saying his brain is permanently fried."

No one said a word about Riley. Apparently, I was the only one who'd noticed the look on his face as Travis went insane. That made sense when I thought about it. No one else had any reason to be looking at Riley at that moment. Even if they happened to glance in his direction, they probably wouldn't recognize the significance of his expression. Only I had reason to be wary of him already.

By the time the 3:35 p.m. bell rang, I couldn't take it anymore. I had to confront him.

Cornering Riley wasn't hard since, as usual, he had chosen the desk directly behind mine. I waited just outside the classroom door, gesturing wordlessly for Vik and Bree to go on without me. Then, when Riley came out, I ambushed him.

"We need to talk," I said bluntly.

Surprise flicked across Riley's face, but a second later, he'd regained his composure.

"Yes?" he asked coolly.

I looked around. The hallway was swarming with students, but Mr. Price was still in his classroom, as most of the teachers would be. In the end, I pulled Riley into a nearby janitor's closet. It seemed faintly ridiculous, discussing such fantastic events surrounded by mops, brooms and various other humble objects, but it was better than the hallway. It was going to be awkward enough without an audience.

"I want to know how you did what you did to Travis, and why," I said.

He looked at me the way you'd look at a poodle that suddenly started reciting Hamlet.

"I... I know not what you mean," he said.

"Don't lie to me!" I snapped. "I saw the way you were looking at him."

Riley's lip curled. "That's your damning evidence?" he sneered. "That I looked at him?"

My cheeks flushed. Now that I'd said it aloud, it sounded ridiculous. But my gut was still telling me Riley was to blame.

"It had to be you," I protested weakly. "Who else could have done something like that?"

"I think you'll find the question is not who, but what. The boy foolishly ingested a most potent drug, or so believe the authorities."

I shook my head. "That doesn't add up. There were a hundred people at that party, and none of them saw Travis take drugs."

"Perhaps he did so while hiding in the lavatory."

"Or perhaps he didn't take anything at all," I said mockingly.

Riley only smiled patronizingly at me.

"I suggest you leave the detective work to the police, Miss Slate. You clearly have no aptitude for it."

He started to walk out of the room. Furious, I called after him, "That's not all I've seen you do!"

He froze, his hand on the doorknob.

The next instant, I found myself pushed up against the closet wall. Riley was gripping me by the shoulders, his face so close to mine that I could practically count the eyelashes framing his unearthly eyes.

"What do you mean?" he demanded, his hot breath warming my cheeks. I was seriously freaked out, but there was no turning back now.

"Last week, in the parking lot at Henrietta's," I said. "You just vanished. I only took my eyes off of you for a second. No normal person could have run away that fast."

For the first time, Riley Bay was at a loss for words. I would have smiled triumphantly if I wasn't so scared of what he might do next.

"And that's not even taking into account the weird way you talk, or the fact that your past is a complete mystery, or—" I stopped short. I didn't want to tell Riley that I'd seen him in my dreams. That seemed too... intimate. He might get the wrong idea.

"You... you noticed these things?"

"Of course. I'm not blind."

He shook his head. "But you're just a girl. One utterly insignificant girl. How could you...?"

Riley trailed off. He was looking at me in a completely different way then: with wonder and—was it possible?—a touch of fear.

"Perhaps the prophecy is true, after all," he murmured, more to himself than to me.

"What prophecy?" I asked, baffled.

Riley just stared at me some more. The gears in his head were clearly turning a mile a minute, but I couldn't guess what they were producing. Finally, he seemed to come to a decision.

"They'll never believe you," he said. "They'll think you've been ingesting drugs as well."

I opened my mouth, then closed it again. He was right. If I was really the only person who'd noticed all of the strange things about Riley Bay, then trying to tell people would be pointless. They'd find it much easier to believe that I'd gone insane than that I'd actually witnessed any of it.

Riley finally released his viselike grip on my shoulders.

"Go home, little girl," he said. "Enjoy your mundane little life while you still can."

And with that, he was gone.

THE NEW NEW ULTRA WEIRD

SILK AND STEEL, AN EXCERPT
RON MILLER

Ron Miller (born May 8, 1947 in Minneapolis, Minnesota) is an artist and author who lives and works in South Boston, Virginia in the United States. His fiction is perhaps the finest specimen of the New New Ultra Weird's capacity for the sublime. The following is an intricate weaving of poetry and prose so assiduous and picaresque in its execution that the difference between both forms is blurred. In these next pages you will find, dear reader, an erotic liberation of metaphor that raises base instinct from its prurient interests to a grandiose height of symbolism. Reader discretion is advised.

As Spikenard watched, Bronwyn slipped the transparent cloak from her shoulders; it fell with a whisper. She let her hands drop to her sides; she pulled her shoulders back and stood erect, feet apart, legs straight. This is what he saw:

Bronwyn standing pale and tall in the nervous light that shimmered through a vibrating canopy of green leaves. The shifting bands of milky light and emerald shadow made her seem luminous, translucent, as though she were a tallow candle glowing beneath its own flame. Like a porcelain lantern. Like a curtain fluttering in a window at dawn. Like a ghost that came and went with the twilight and darkness, that first veiled and then revealed.

Her hair had the sheen of the sea beneath an eclipsed moon. It was the color of a leopard's tongue, of oiled mahogany. It was terra cotta, bay and chestnut. Her hair was a helmet, a hood, the cowl of the monk, magician or cobra. Her face had the fragrance of a gibbous moon. The scent of fresh snow. Her eyes were dark birds in fresh snow. They were the birds' shadows, they were mirrors; they were the legends on old charts. They were antique armor and the tears of dragons. Her brows were a raptor's sharp, anxious wings. They were a pair of scythes. Her ears were a puzzle carved in ivory. Her teeth were her only bracelet; she carried them within the red velvet purse of her lips. Her tongue was amber. Her tongue was a ferret, an anemone, a tux caught in the teeth of a tiger.

Her shoulders were the clay in a potter's kiln. Her shoulders were fieldstones; they were the white, square stones of which walls are made. They were windows covered with steam. They were porcelain. They were opal and moonstone. Her neck was the foam that curls from the prow of a ship, it was a sheaf of alfalfa or barley, it was the lonely dance of the pearl-grey shark.

Her legs were quills. They were bundles of wicker, they were candelabra; the muscles were summer lightning, that flickered like a passing thought; they were captured eels or a cable on a windlass. Her thighs were geese, pythons, schooners. They were cypress or banyan; her thighs were a forge, they were shears; her thighs were sandstone, they were the sandstone buttresses of a cathedral, they were silk or cobwebs. Her calves were sweet with the sap of elders, her feet were bleached bone, her feet were driftwood. Her feet were springs, marmosets or locusts; her toes were snails, they were snails with shells of tears. Her arms were a corral, a fence, an enclosure; they were pennants; they were highways. Her fingers were incense. They were silver fish in clear water, they were the speed of the fish, they were the fish's wake. They were semaphores; they were meteors.

Her spine was a snake. It was the track Of a snake. It was the groove the water snake makes in the glossy mud of the riverbank. Her spine was a viper, an anaconda. It was the strength of the anaconda. It was the anaconda's unknown hieroglyphic. Her spine was a ladder, a rod; it was a chain, a canal, it was a caravan. Her buttocks were fresh-baked loaves; they were ivory eggs, they were the eggs of the lonely phoenix. They were a fist.

Her breasts were citrus, they were soapstone; they were bright cumulus and the smooth fingertips of Musrum. Her breasts were honeycombs and dew-beaded windows, or soft, sweet cheese. They were sweet apples; they were glass, they were cowries. They were the twin moons of the earth. The nipples rose like mercury with her heat. They rose like monuments atop flowered hills, above deserts of hot sand; the nipples were savory morels, with the flavor of the forest.

Her ribs were a niche, an alcove, an apse; her stomach was an idol in the niche, alcove or apse, an effigy, a phantom. Her stomach was a beach, a savannah, a flagstone warmed by the sun, a cat asleep on the flagstone, a bleached canvas sail in hot southern winds. Her navel winked like a doll's eye, like the eye of a whale, like the drowsy cat.

Her pubes was a field of wheat after the harvest, a field neatly furrowed; it was a nest, a pomegranate, an arrowhead, a rune. It was a shadow. It was moss on a smooth white stone. There was an orchid within the moss. There was a drop or dew upon the orchid. It had the breath of moss beds, of the deep seas, of the abyss, of scrimshaw and blue glass, of cold iron; she had the sex of rain forests, the ibis and the scarab; she had the sex of mirrors and candles, of the hot, careful winds that stroke the veldt, the winds that taste of clay and seed and blood; the winds that dreamed of tawny, lean animals.

"You are quite beautiful, Princess Bronwyn," Spikenard sang, with his sardonic grin and eyes as violet and hard as amethysts. "Your body is halfway between earth and dream, neither magic nor elemental, neither animal nor spirit."

His long fingers reached toward her face, brushed her eyelids...

"Your eyes are the sound of rain."

... followed the contours of her cheekbones and jaw...

"Chalkbeds and moonlight..."

...down her neck, like curious spiders...

"Bottles of wine, covered with dew, and otters."

...touched the sharp ridges of her collarbones, the hollow at the base of her throat... circled her domed breasts like moths orbiting a pair of glowing lamps.

The glade had grown dark, a resonant iron-blackness that was filled with swarming fireflies and luminous eyes, curious constellations that formed and re-formed, focusing on their center of gravity, the binary Star at the center of their universe: Bronwyn and Spikenard.

Spikenard shone like a bar of silver at a blue heat, he shone so that he gave off sparks. He circled Bronwyn like a pinwheel, a comet, cocooning her in his lambent trail. Bronwyn, too, had become luminous, glowing like an ingot of iron in a blacksmith's forge.

He spoke to her but all she heard was music, and his scent filled her head like a wineskin. Her nerves resonated in symphony and her body swayed and turned with his orbits, like a compass following, a magnet. Her mouth and tongue were as dry as flannel, they burned like a furnace, yet her body was beaded with sweat like a glass of cold wine. The beads coalesced and ran down her arms and sides, down the groove of her spine, funneled between her breasts, in rivulets that tickled like the lick of a hundred tiny tongues. Sequins of perspiration ringed her lips, and her tongue lapped at the salty fluid.

Spikenard touched her as he circled, he touched and stroked and caressed as quickly and gently as the lighting of a fly. His long fingers, like Tudela's tubes of glowing gas, stroked the princess at random, each touch leaving a luminous trail, each touch causing Bronwyn to shudder and gasp, as though she had been shocked. His fingers ran down her spine and her stomach rippled like a flag, they fluttered up her thighs and she convulsed and bit her lip, they brushed her nipples and she clenched her hands so tightly her nails bit Into her palms, they touched her lips and she moaned and nipped at them, but they had moved on. The long fingers danced on her buttocks and slid down the crease between them, and the muscles of Bronwyn's legs stood out like hungry anacondas.

She was no longer aware of any world outside the swirling cylinder Of light that was Spikenard; he seemed to be at one and the same time on all sides of her and motionless in front of her; his hands had become multiplicitous, yet they held her face; his tongue licked at her soles, the small of her back, plumbed the well of her navel, yet his sardonic smile never left her sight; he bit at her shoulders, her ears, at the insides of her thighs, yet his steady eyes held hers as though they were slivers of glass driven through her head.

His song to her throbbed and hummed like an oboe and her heart raced in accompaniment like the drumroll preceding a blindfolded circus high diver.

She lifted from the ground, weightless by her own ecstasy, rising like a spark from her own furnace. She grasped Spikenard's phallus with both hands, and it burnt like a bar of red-hot iron: she cried out from the pain, but held on with the pleasure of it. Something parted in her groin, like lips parting for a kiss, and she felt a viscid moistness wet her thighs; she could smell the scent of her own musk and her nostrils flared and her tongue tasted the air like a snake's. The bristly mound of her pubes buzzed and hummed like a shaken hornet's nest. She threw her head back and the cords of her neck stood out like taut wires, her eyes were open wide and Spikenard's sardonic face filled her vision, each violet eye a mirror reflecting her own face, distorted by the curved lens, distorted by her rapture. His face pressed against hers, the wetness of his lips mingled with the perspiration on her mouth, his tongue circled hers like an eel, and his breath tasted of cinnamon and nutmeg.

"Spikenard!" The name cut through the atmosphere like a white-hot spike thrust into a crystal sphere. There was a shattering sound and the faerie king turned his face away from the rhapsodized princess.

It was Seremonth who had called, and who now stood, legs apart, arms akimbo, fists clenched, her eyes like incombustible spheres of iron within the flame of her face and body. Her wings caught her incandescence and reflected sheets of magenta and electric blue that swirled around her like aurorae.

Spikenard released Bronwyn, who swayed like a metronome, eyes as empty as cups. He turned to his rebellious wife with a sardonic smile and murderous eyes.

"You have gotten a power," he observed.

"Oh, yes I have!" affirmed the faerie queen.

"Why do you interrupt me?"

"Leave the human alone!"

"Why? Doesn't she deserve a reward for saving us?"

"Who's getting the reward, you or her?"

"We're not jealous, are we?"

"And if I am?"

"You seem to forget who I am, Seremonth," he reminded her quietly. "It's not like you to make mistakes like that."

"You seem to have forgotten who I am: a bigger mistake."

"You imply that I am to suffer somehow from this?"

"Release the human; you are offering her no reward and you know that. She would have no memory of this, except in her dreams, and they would haunt and disturb her all her life. You said yourself that she has done you no harm; unlike any human before, she has helped you. Why do this to her?"

"Because I wish to!"

"Then I shall release her!"

"No!"

Seremonth burst with light, and Bronwyn cartwheeled across the wet moss, coming to rest in a jointless heap. Though drenched with perspiration, she no longer flamed and the moistness quickly grew chill; steamed in the cool air. Her sodden hair matted to her face and shoulders like clay, but when she lifted her head from the moss her eyes were clear and intelligent.

What she first took to be a fireworks display, she realized was a pair of faeries in mortal combat: Spikenard and Seremonth. She fully recollected what had been happening to her and, a little unsteadily as yet, took advantage of the distracted king to attempt an exit.

Behind her, powerful faerie king threw his opponent to the ground, her wings shattered and her luminous body guttering like an exhausted candle. He rose from the semiconscious queen and turned, when he saw the distant figure of the princess breaking through the ferns and stalks at the far side of the arena.

"Bronwyn!"

She looked back at the sound of her name. She saw violet eyes that flamed like aurorae and a tall figure that stepped from the distant shadows. She stood her ground, not hypnotized as before, but with the resolve to see through whatever was coming. Legs braced, fists clenched, shoulders back, chin down. She saw grinning teeth glowing like embers in a furnace. The breath glowed and sparkled, and hissing steam hit her in the face. "Watch, human!" the steam said

A firefly light lit a circular space between them, and she watched.

Blood-red hands danced in the ivory light like ecstatic spiders; fluttering harvestmen that jerked and flickered While strangely intricate patterns and devices appeared in soil and pebble. The spider-legs pirouetted and gamboled, scratching webs in the circle of light, to a nerveless tune invented a millennium earlier. Tiny vials of colored liquid appeared, joined the gavotte and there was a splash here and a dab there and a strange intimation of order was suggested. Then the pattern was finished and the spiders again were hands.

A quiver shook one of the particles of dust near the center of the circle. It quivered again and it was a golden mite, a brazen toy gnat with tin wings and a clockwork body. It gave a clicking jump into the air and hopped and puffed from gnat to mosquito to fly to shining, golden bee. In a quick series of jerks it became as large as a hummingbird, though very much different in form and color (already she could see a tiny tufted tail and that it stood on four sturdy legs).

Then, as quickly as a balloon inflated at a vendor's tank, and with much the same hiss and squeak, the gryphon was as large as a Great Dane. Bronwyn felt the recoil from a sharp glance of molten copper eyes, before a final burst flung the monster to its full height, far above her head. She held breath and heart still in utter, utter awe. The gryphon's own breath rumbled and thundered like a distant storm while sparkling steam hissed from its nostrils as though from a charged Bessemer converter. Archangel eyes and nervous wings. Wings like a metalsmith's dream: plated lace, platinum feathers, brass scales of an Ibrailan intricacy. It had lightning for muscles and thunder for flesh and the gryphon looked at the faerie king only.

"Seize her!" he ordered in voice that exploded in Bronwyn's brain. And it obeyed.

Its steel claws had enveloped her like a cage when, with a shriek like a steam locomotive, the gryphon disintegrated. Bronwyn was scooped from the earth, tumbling into a huge, soft hollow, and the pit of her stomach wrenched with the sensation of rising rapidly. She looked up and for the one dizzying moment before she lost consciousness she saw, towering above her like a mountain, the abundant, boundless, heaven-crowned figure of Thud Mollockle.

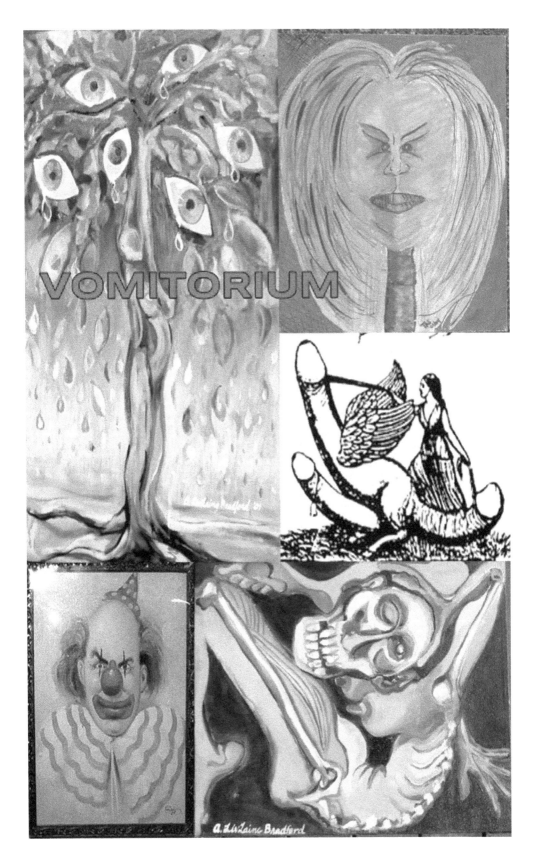

THE NEW NEW ULTRA WEIRD

BEING BORN
BERTRAND RUSSELL

T HE ROOM IS ALL WHITE, blindingly so. In the center of the room sits a fish bowl atop a small table. Simple and round, made of clear glass. A quiet and high toned beep emits from somewhere. A man wearing a black suit holding a briefcase enters. The glint of his gold watch chain reflects elegantly as he approaches the table.

He sets the briefcase down. The click of a latch, the squeak of latex gloves. A small eye dropper emerges in hand. Moments pass. He silently stares into the clear glass bowl, catching the reflection of his face atop the surface of the water. Carefully he fills the dropper from the vial and brings it above the bowl. Extending his arm at an upward angle, he lets a single drop fall. A ripple moves across the small surface of water. The man in the suit quickly stows the vial back into the briefcase. He stands for a moment, looking slightly impatient. There is another small tone, and he exits.

The fish bowl sits.

Slowly, a ruby-colored film begins to form at the surface, spreading to the rims of the glass. Long red veins extend down into the depth of the bowl and intertwine, as if consciously taking shape and form. The intertwined strands harden and become solid matter. Then as if vines on a wall, more stands twist and grow atop these hardened structures. A figure is now recognizable. Muscle structure and organs take shape from the nothingness. Slowly these are covered by a growing translucent skin, which slowly becomes more opaque. Eyes, at first milky and unresponsive, become light-sensitive. Staring out from the bowl, the pupils begin to respond and fluctuate. Hanging like fruit on a tree, an unborn child is suspended within the fishbowl.

The tiny figure begins to move, becoming conscious and aware. There is a sudden lurch from the child, the fishbowl splashes a bit on the table. Two small hands reach out from the waters surface, gently gripping the rim of the container. Using his own strength, the child pulls itself from the bowl, and comes down upon the table with a wet thud. The back of the arms and legs are still connected to ruby vines, running up and pumping in a knotted mass within the bowl. The child is motionless for a few minutes, breathing. Then, with the confidence and form of a grown man, the babe stands up. Looking down at its own body, it frees its arms and legs from the tangles.

"Another boy," is heard over a distant loudspeaker.

The boy effectively scales from table to chair, and from chair to floor. He begins to walk around the perimeter of the room. His arms are folded behind his back.

"Bring in the toy trucks," said the voice from the loudspeaker.

A small, two-foot panel raises itself on the far side of the room. An abundance of multicolored remote trucks trundle in, to the point where they fill half the floor space of the room. Small monitors flip up on the trucks, the smiling faces of various musicians, instruments in hand. The babe raises his brow in interest, thinks a moment, and then gives a slight nod. Climbing back up the chair and onto the table, he peers down over the proud faces of his toy truck assembly. A panel opens on the ceiling and down drops a wire, on the end of which a slender baton is fastened. The babe grabs the baton with the utmost bravado and swirls it through the air above his head. Then, standing firm for a moment, eyes closed, he taps the baton to the table twice. At his cue, the small trucks begin to perform.

DOGGY DOO
DAISY STARCHILD

TYLER ROLLED OVER and looked at the pile of brown stuff smashed into the ground. His face scrunched up when he realized what it was and a barely audible groan escaped his small mouth.

As he eased himself off the ground, his brother's dog, Apollo came ambling over. Apollo lapped his tongue up the side of Tyler's face. Tyler tried to push him away and sneak back inside before his mom caught him.

The day began as any other for six-year-old Tyler. He crawled off the top bunk of his bed, careful not to make any noise. The last thing he wanted was his brother waking up. That would definitely ruin his Saturday.

He poured himself a bowl of cereal, dumping half the box on the cool auburn tiles of the kitchen floor. After pouring some milk over the flakes, he headed for the living room, sloshing more cereal along the way. Watching cartoons was Tyler's plan for the day, and he didn't anticipate any interruptions.

Two hours of cartoons was all Tyler could manage to watch. The house started stirring and the mess he made was discovered.

"Tyler!" his mom called.

His head turned slowly toward the doorway of the living room, the fear sliding across his features.

"Tyler!" she called again, the agitation evident in her voice.

Tyler jumped out of the chair and started toward the kitchen, Apollo close on his heels.

"What is this Tyler?"

The little kid hesitated. "I thought Apollo might be hungry?" His statement came out in the form of a question, completely unsure of the forthcoming reaction.

"You know the rules. If you can't do something yourself, you have to ask for help. And, if you make a mess, you have to clean it up."

Tyler's shoulders slumped.

"Timeout. In your room. Let's go."

"How long?" he moaned.

"I'll come get you. And don't you dare wake your brother up."

Tyler sulked back through the house to his brother's dark, depressing bedroom. Although it was a bright and sunny fall day, you couldn't tell from that room. The turquoise blinds were closed, cutting off the little sunlight actually able to penetrate the miniscule bedroom Tyler slept in.

He quietly shut the door behind him and ambled up the ladder to his little fort. The room was equipped with an ancient, window-sized air conditioner, but the air was still stifling. Tyler curled himself up in the corner of his top bunk, practically hugging the wall. He picked up his favorite glow-in-the-dark *Thomas the Tank Engine* book, which he kept tucked beneath his pillow. This was the only solace he knew in the dreary room he called home. Sharing a room with a brother six years older was no cake walk.

Adam chose the paint color a few years earlier—a dark, claustrophobia-inducing turquoise, which matched the blinds. The boys shared a bunk bed which sat against the only unobstructed wall in the room. The bed was so big that there was just enough room left to open the door all the way. Tyler was stuck on the top bunk and Adam got the bottom. This was primarily because Adam was older and got to choose, but it might have had something to do with the time Tyler played with the bed rail and Adam fell off the top in the middle of the night. Having to climb up to the top bunk and back down every single day made Tyler dismal, especially because that was really the only space he could call his own. He did everything he could to make his top bunk more suited for the six-year-old he was. There were Scooby-Doo and Thomas the Tank Engine posters held to the cracked and dirty, off-white ceiling with silly putty. A picture of his mom and a plaque about firefighting from his dad rounded out the collection in his little fort, adding a personal touch to such an impersonal space. The only other item in the room he could call his own was the small pine dresser he was stuck with when his mom finally gave his twin sister her own. There wasn't room for anything else. Since Adam was older, he got more stuff and he was, in essence, in charge—at least in their bedroom.

The rest of this small, dark room was filled with Adam's furniture. The cold, hard, pine floorboards were uninviting on winter mornings. Luckily, there wasn't much there to walk on since the floor space left in the room was just big enough for one, maybe two, people to stand in. The large, low-set, dark brown dresser was overbearing and the wall space was monopolized by movie posters and firefighter memorabilia. Tyler hated spending time in his bedroom. It was like living in someone else's world, afraid to leave your mark for fear of being caught.

After a half hour of reading and rereading the book about Thomas, Tyler's brother Adam finally rolled out of bed and staggered into the other room. Tyler peered over the edge of his bed and watched his older, bigger brother exit none too quietly. Once the door was closed again, Tyler lifted the blinds behind his head to let some light in. He crawled out of bed and grabbed a few more books from the top of his dresser before hunkering down for the long haul.

It seemed like all day passed before Tyler heard his name called from the depths of the house. When he did finally hear something, he sat up slowly, wondering if it was a dream. A minute later, he heard it again and knew he was actually supposed to move. Setting his book aside and peeling his teddy bear blanket away (a Christmas gift from his mother), he crawled to the edge of his bunk and shimmied down the ladder.

Cracking the door ever so slightly, he called back, "Yeah?"

"Would you come here please?"

Hesitantly he opened the door farther and stepped out, closing it behind him. He looked around the corner to find his dad simultaneously playing Solitaire on the computer and watching some college football game on the television. Adam was engrossed in the game as well. Apollo was curled up on the floor next to the couch, taking his morning nap. So much for watching more cartoons.

Tyler skipped past the living room, through the dining room and stopped dead in the kitchen. The look on his mother's face told him he wasn't scot free, off on good behavior.

"Go pick up our toys and put some shoes and your jacket on. I need help outside"

"But Mom," he pleaded, "it's cold outside. Why can't Adam or Megan do it?"

"First of all, it's a beautiful day outside. The fresh air will do you some good. And second of all, Adam and Megan didn't dump their cereal all over the house this morning. Now let's go. I can't waste my whole Saturday waiting for you."

"Fine," he grumbled before stalking off to the living room again.

Tyler walked to the far end of the living room and stood in front of the television, picking up his hot wheels. He put the cars in their container, taking his sweet time. He crumpled up the play mat, tossing both in the corner.

"Move your butt, Moron," Adam sneered.

Tyler turned around and stuck his tongue out. He was certain a chase would ensue, but decided to do it anyway. He made it around the coffee table and past his dad before Adam caught up. Adam grabbed Tyler by the back of his shirt; Tyler tried to keep moving forward, but Adam was bigger and stronger, keeping him from going anywhere. In an instant, Tyler had been tackled to the ground, the carpet scraping his face. Adam took a seat on top of him and continued to watch the game. After he let a fart go, Adam got up and sauntered back to the chair, not letting his eyes stray from the television set. Their dad didn't say a word; he didn't even look up from the computer screen. Tyler pulled himself to his feet and ran around the corner to his bedroom.

He put on his boots, not bothering with any socks, and dug a sweatshirt out of his dresser. The one he grabbed was a new one his mom had bought for school. He knew he should probably put it back and grab some old one that he'd worn for years, but at the moment, Tyler just didn't care. While standing in his room, he wanted to mess with Adam's stuff, but he knew he had to sleep in there that night, and his bedtime was way before Adam's. In the end, it didn't seem like a good idea to even stir a speck of dust.

Once outfitted in appropriate clothes for the crisp fall weather, Tyler went to meet his mother. He could have taken the door out to the garage or even gone out the front and walked around the house, but Tyler was feeling adventurous. In the dining room he pulled a chair to the wall and climbed on top. He pushed and pulled at the window until he got it all the way up. He put one leg through the hole, straddling the sill. Tyler looked down and got nervous, but kept going. He tried to pull his other leg out to just jump to the ground, but he wasn't that flexible. Before he could stop himself, he was falling to the grass, four feet from the bottom of the window.

When he landed, Tyler felt something squish on his back. He rolled over into a pile of crisp fall leaves his mother just raked, crunching them to smithereens, and looked at where he had just landed. A pile of Apollo's poop was mashed into the long, wet grass.

FALLEN ANGEL
STRETCH ARMSTRONG

PROLOGUE

AM A FALLEN ANGEL who wished to plunge a flaming blade into the heart of that suffering devil, as I kissed him with more love and anger than should be possible in all of creation. As I felt his fingers run through my hair, and down my back I struck him with my knife. I could feel it plunge into his heart. I saw his tears stream down his face as he realized it was I who betrayed him. His eyes penetrated my soul. He ripped it apart trying to find the cause of my betrayal. When he kissed me with his last breath, his lips soaked with tears of sorrow, I was broken from my trance. This kiss would burn me forever. I saw what I had done; my soul was crushed.

I had to know why! I spread my wings and flew up to heaven. Peter would not let me enter, for my sins held me back. I beat and clawed at the Pearly Gates for *seven* days. I did not rest on the seventh. Heaven stood in shock of my rebellion, but I was too torn to notice. God appeared before me and demanded to know the meaning of my rebellion. I related the story between sobs and tears, begging her to reverse it, to bring him back and to forgive me for taking an innocent life with my fiery sword. She said that I wanted him dead, not consciously, but subconsciously, so that I could have another that I had always wanted and needed. I refused to believe it, and called her a liar! For this, she told me who that one was and cast me into the lake of fire to burn in misery and loneliness. My soul would be tormented for eternity, not for guilt, but for regret and loss. She told me I could have had her because she wanted me— her creation! She hid this secret in the box of Pandora, and took my ability to speak the name. I could never tell anyone who it was that desired me because the truth would shake the elements, reality, and all the creation! Finally, it would destroy heaven.

God rejected me from heaven. She had casted me down with all her strength. I plummeted to earth as if I were a flash of light. At this speed, I flickered through dimensions; I saw glimpses of the heaven I once knew. A realm of over whelming love, a place of happiness, and all the dreams a person could have come true. I saw views of earth: a cold, dark and wicked place with the sins of men, as they destroy each other in the name of a loving God, who was kind to her creation, or so I once thought. I saw worst of all the hell that was before me, a furnace of undying tortures that even the most hateful, wicked of men could not conjure.

I discovered that every bone in an angel's body could break, as they were split and crushed by every layer of rock I struck. With ease, I blasted through the earth's mantle and into the river of heat beneath the earth; this was the last portal-dimension into hell. Once an all-loving God casts you from heaven, you can only be damned. Damnation was the ironic price for my own love, and loss of that love had sealed my fate. Revenge against the God that cursed me was my penance. Only through vengeance and justice can I recover what I had lost: the lover I was forced to betray.

one

Who am I? How long have I been in such a wretched world? My hair has over-grown; I have a face that feels grained in my hands. It is strange that I have never seen my face. I answer my life to a beast with singed, muddy wings. They say I have only one god and he is called *The Prince*. I believe I am in hell. The heat is unbearable. I die every day from the torture and agony. This is my only time for peace: the silence of death. I look forward to this horrific, dark friend, everyday but it only lasts a moment. My god is no god, whatever it is feeds off misery. I wake to the gruel, sinister laughter of those *beasts*, a name that I've given them. Nothing guards me, only a slave driver watches simply to lavish in my agony.

When my dark friend embraces me I have dreams of a darker place with a beautiful demon. I know the feeling I have with him is unforgiving… but when I wake my heart pulses and lips burn with a lovely sin. It tastes like the salt of tears and the wetness of a kiss as if I truly know what a loving gesture means.

Other poor souls around me pine for their beloved family, but I remember little of anything, only soft kisses, and an unbearable, teasing memory of happiness. Maybe my memories are being replaced by this place, and all I know now is pain. The others say they burn for their guilt, and do not know which hurts more. But I… but I feel no guilt, "why am I here?" I ask myself. I remember no sin. I feel no guilt of wrong transgressions.

I know the key to my memory is my death dreams, the pain in my heart and on my lips. As I thought these things my beast calls, "Lucky damnation! The Prince demands to see you!"

"What would he want with me?" I think to myself.

Another beast hurls a boulder of brimstone at me. "Hurry up before I flay you," he bellows. It takes hold of me by my hair and begins to run, dragging me over smoldering rocks, at great speed. The thing leaps into the air and takes flight; my body helplessly dangles underneath.

The abyss of Hell is so expansive that even above all else I can't see the end. Nothing is in sight except barren fire lands, nothing can be heard but the screams of those being tortured till their souls leap from their bodies. They look mutilated, twisted and contorted. Nothing looked the way it was meant to look. Nothing looked like a creation from a God of love. These wretched souls can only breathe sulfur, and will never know relief.

We fly, although it never seems as if we move, and before us appears a large structure, a castle of bone. The peaks of the skeleton castle reach out and pierce the bloodied sky. No windows could be seen in this fortress. It erupts from the floor of hell with a kind of putrid organic stature. As we come closer to this tormenting monument the beast releases me carelessly from his grasp and I plummet to the sharp rocks below. All I can do is brace for the impact. I collided with the sharp peaks and as they cut and tear my flesh. I awake to find myself embedded into the hot surface of the ground. I formed a crater before the entryway.

"Come in boy, we have business to discuss" came a hollowed voice from inside.

I stagger to my feet. Looking at the Prince's" kingdom before his castle, I knew I had no chance of escape; my only choice was to continue. Upon entering the home, I was taken by surprise because the interior was familiar, I have been here before, but I don't know when. The floor has a glossy texture. It is laid with diamond shaped tiles, having the appearance of a distorted chessboard. The walls are translucent one moment, opaque the next. There are creatures in some of the walls, living trophies. The creatures are unable to move, and will look at the adjacent walls until the end of time. That is true madness.

A squatty rotund demon appears behind me—I assume he is a servant of the master because of his upright posture and commanding voice— "my name is Ruundul. The master is waiting." He begins walking toward the wall. When it becomes translucent he beckons, "come along now."

With hesitation, I follow not knowing what to expect. I emerge on the other side of the wall and Ruundal is gone. I am standing alone in a chamber with the structure design of a cathedral, only the crosses are inverted. Stain glass windows depict demonic victories. I feel a horrible chill.

A figure rises from the floor's east corner.

"Who are you?" I am shaken, and ask this visibly anxious.

TWO

"That is the perfect question! And to be frank, you should know who I am. The figures size doubles with this remark.

This was my first verification, I had known were I was before but it helped for someone that wasn't being burned alive to admit it to me. "Who are you?" I ask again firmly.

"This is my office, who do you think I am?" he states coolly.

"I can take a guess if you'd like?" I am trying to refuse him the satisfaction of fame.

He stops walking away and turns in a playful manner. "You're joking right? Are you naïve? Look around you, and tell me who *I am*".

The room is lit like the grand study of a Vatican cleric. Books are everywhere. There are endless rows of literature. He begins to walk to his desk, which is made of what appears to be polished obsidian. The legs are fashioned into lion's paws. He reaches his desk, and as he sits a massive fireplace appears behind him, casting a haunting glow over his face. His clothing wasn't what you would expect from such a powerful... Whatever he was. He wore a suit with no jacket and his tie said 'flame broiled'.

"So you know why you are here right?" he inquires.

"I really have no idea."

He gives me a disappointed glance. "Oh, I figured it would be obvious since the 'Bitch upstairs' threw you out like a dead-beat husband."

"Excuse me? What do you mean 'bitch upstairs'?" I retort with a flush of heat through my body. I'm furious that he has me in such a vulnerable position, but remain composed

He leans forward in his high-back office chair, like he is a CEO of some major company, and stares at me.

"Are you Fucking with me!?" he fumes.

The fireplace burst outward into the room, surrounding me in a cage of embers. For some reason I feel no fear at this, and he notices. Soon the flames dissipate. He takes a deep breath, and chuckles warmly.

"I'm sorry about that my boy. I was told by my helper, Ruundul, that you were someone that I needed," he says with relaxed tone.

"I'm sorry but I don't remember anything that may help you, all I remember is waking up here, "I reply in an overly desperate tone.

"Really," he said in a flat voice, "Maybe we can jog your memory." He walks toward me and says, "No matter how much this hurts don't take your eyes off mine" He takes hold of my neck and thrusts his fingers into my forehead, the pain is unbearable. I keep eye contact until a blinding light envelopes my vision, I black out.

THree

"She fucked with your head pretty bad, here eat a cookie," he says, handing me a plate with little teddy bear designs on it. He probably took it from a sweet little grandmother's house. I look over from the soft couch I am now laying on and see him over a stove. He is humming while he bakes in a 'kiss the cook' apron.

"Where am I?" I stammer.

"Oh, a cottage in the Appellation Mountains, some old fart croaked like a toad and, well, I figured you'd enjoy a feel of Earth." He responds in a pleasant tone that seems both friendly and chilling.

"An old fart croaked? Have a little respect for the deceased." I scoff.

"Oh, and you're one to talk? We have business to care for and I'll apologize to the old grams when I get home, does that make you happy?" He retorts mockingly.

Chills run down my spine. "What do you mean, 'I'm one to talk?'" I say in a fearful inquiry.

"You have your memory; I'll jog it for yah. You are the Angel of Death. You've been *killing people* for well... an eternity. Until you came knocking at my door anyway."

—He is suggesting that the morality killing is not dependent on intent. That it is all the same. —

The memories do come flooding back, the kiss, the blade, the excruciating pain I feel in my chest. I can't believe what I have done! What she made me do!

"It's all there now isn't it? Bet you're pissed, huh?" His face now painted with a toothy grin.

I scream. The pitch vibrates some cups on the table.

"Quiet down. You'll wake the dead," he finds that one way funnier than it is.

I realize he is comfortably in his own little world. I guess being in hell since the beginning would do that. "I have a business offer; I'll be blunt because I know you're in a lot of pain. I want to kill God." His blunt words are striking.

"Wow. That's quite an order." The humor of his wish gives me security. I feel at an advantage for once in this exchange, for a moment.

"Oh, my boy, you'd be *amazed* at the little white lies *She* spreads. After all it is in Her favor....you'll be shocked at what you can do to a god.

"This is my plan."— As if I actually am behind him on this—

"I want to build your strength back, you still have a touch of that heavenly might,. I'm going to teach you how to wield the powers of hell and then, together, we're going to take on The Most High! What do you think?" He stands erect, smiling like a child.

"I think you're certifiable."

"Oh you think so? After what she did to you! I thought you, of all creatures, would want retribution against your creator. I mean after all she killed your lover, out of childish jealousy and damned you to hell for simply rejecting her advances on you...How can that go unpunished? Other than her, we are the most powerful of all creation. We *can* do this! Then I, second only to her, will be given my rightful place on the throne and I can bring your love back again. What do you say, partner?"

"Sure why not."

THE NEW NEW ULTRA WEIRD

Black and White and Read

Lisa Napertmente

BEAUTIFUL. I WOKE UP one morning, and my whole room had changed color. Cerulean sheets and opalesque pillowcase. My blanket, though it once was onyx, had changed to fuscia. I woke up inundated with hue and surrounded by light.

I walked downstairs. Every step changed with my footsteps: violet, sienna, veridian. The colors blended, breathed, and swirled like a tye-dye kaleidoscope. I looked behind my path and saw tinted footprints. I thought, *How did this happen to me? More importantly, why?*

I took off all of my clothes and sat on my couch. I thought of vermillion and projected it through the tips of my fingers. I thought of ochre, and ochre happened upon what I touched.

Although these colors were beautiful, I wondered why. *What makes colors beautiful? Why do we call colors names? What right do we have to give a name to the light that gave us life?* This gave me an idea.

I walked outside and thought of only darkness. I touched the grass outside of my house and made it black. Then I touched the shutters, which shuddered with a dismal emptiness. I touched the windows, and I made them blackboard glass. I went through the whole town and touched everyone's geraniums and chrysanthemums. I touched traffic lights, cars, cats: forcing it all to black. *Color is a lie*, I thought. *The truth lies where images can't get in our way.* Everything became indistinguishable from everything else.

In piled news reports of a mysterious naked woman who caused darkness wherever she went. They called me evil, but they didn't know that their curiosity, their need to classify the world into a spectrum of color, that was evil. We lie to ourselves and call it green. We lie to our children and call it pink. Color classifies us. *What's your favorite— Why is your girl wearing blue— Why'd you choose to paint your room* that *color—*

After my town was colored with blackness, and white and black men and women no longer knew the difference, I moved to the next town. I touched light bulbs and fire trucks, lanterns and the fire in them. I covered the county in cataclysmic dark.

The national news called me an epidemic. The reports told me I was a terrorist. Writers wrote about me, politicians told their followers I was plague, and their followers believed them.

After two months, I changed the entire country to black. I never told anyone what I was doing. Their lives had been filled with lies for too long, and I would never be able to explain myself in a way that wasn't a lie. I walked to Washington D.C. and blackened monuments. The Hollywood sign disappeared into the black of the hillside—also my doing. Mount Rushmore was just as much nothingness as what we come from.

World leaders sent out orders for my detainment. "The Black Fear," they called me. "Scourge" said the United Nations. But that was alright. How could they find me if they didn't know who I was? Where I was? I was an enigma to the world.

I walked back to my house after I was done with the United States. I then saw that, though America has blackened, I had left my home the way I first changed it. Vermillion sofa, tye-dye footprints, cerulean sheets. I saw these colors and I realized why we lie.

Then, I recolored the country.

DISENCHANTED ENCHANTMENT

QUENTIN NELSON

W E WERE ACCUSTOMED to seeing one another with three-foot beards on four-foot bodies, with rusted hauberks and robes that smelled like dusty tomes, with pointed ears and glowing eyes, with blazing hands and staves that grew green leaves; and as I walked across an LAX terminal I wondered if anyone would recognize me, or I them, because I was twice as tall and half as heavy as my dwarven character.

I didn't wonder for very long. A couple piled onto a nearby escalator: a woman, leaning on a pink suitcase, running her mouth into the ear of the man on the step below, who carried her other pink bag under his arm. The voices of *Littlecheese* and *Bigcheese* that I'd grown accustomed to hearing over the years fit perfectly into the shape of the woman's yammering and the man's feigned responses, respectively, as the man scanned the crowd around baggage claim. When the man spotted me and smiled, I knew that I'd found Robert and Amy.

"Robert?" My tongue was still foreign to my guild leader's name.

"Ralph?" He was adjusting to my name as well.

I smiled so fully I thought I'd carved into my face. We settled for shaking hands but I wanted to embrace him. We'd been friends for five years and I'd never once seen his face. His wife *Littlecheese* --

Amy, now -- had no such hesitation. She shouted "*Orkoth!*" and threw her arms around me to bring me down to her chest in a hug that she had warned me was coming during the Raid earlier that week.

"Its great to meet you too, *Lil',*" I said, muffled by her hair.

"Alright, alright, let him breathe," Robert laughed and placed his hand on her shoulder. He looked at me. "Man, you weren't kidding when you had said you were a little skinnier than *Orkoth.*"

"I didn't help you guys any by shaving my beard," I said pretending to stroke where a three-foot, silver beard might have been."Can't say the same for you. You would be the spitting image of your gnome if you were two-thirds shorter." I was only partially kidding. He couldn't have been much older than thirty, but his hairline was receding, he had very little facial hair, and his glasses were a bit too small for his head -- all attributes that were displayed on the gnome character that he played.

"How do I rack up against *Lil'*? Prettier, wouldn't you say?" Amy said, smiling.

"Why, of course. You've even got the same pointy ears," I said. She was not so immaculately figured as her slender elf, but this was how Amy and I talked, like the flirtations between a man and his girlfriend's mother. Heck, if it weren't for Amy and Robert living in Iowa, and I in New York, Amy would have attempted long ago to pair me with either her daughter my age or the one slightly older.

Before she could even respond we heard the name of our guild shouted from the top of the escalator, "*Disenchanted Enchantment!*" Everyone on the descending stairs looked behind and above at the man accidentally knocking over suitcases and squeezing between couples, excited to reach us. Scott had arrived.

"Holy shit, is that you *Ork*?" Scott said. "How you doing, buddy?"

"Scottyyyyy!" I said as if I'd called him that before. I held out my hand as he came in for a high-five and we ended up bumping shoulders because I thought we were hugging.

Scott was a childhood friend and a co-worker with Robert. Like me, he played a dwarf. Unlike me, he actually looked like a dwarf. He wasn't much taller, he had a red beard that could almost be braided, a belly that was round like a barrel of mead, and a nose that looked chiseled from stone. He and I were the warriors of our guild. We were the ones with the shields, obligated to dive into battle first, to hold the attention of the computer-programmed enemies so that the others like Robert could attack, and hope that healers like Amy would keep us from dying. Twice a week, Scott and I competed for upgraded armaments.

Over the next hour, the four of us grew to a party of nine as all the flights came in. The conversation always began with a comment on everyone's likeness -- or lack thereof -- to their character in-game. More than once, I received looks surprised to see that I was their stalwart shield all these years. But other than these initial exclamations, we refrained from discussing anything related to the game-world. We could do better. We went over when we could check in at the Hyatt, when we could get our passes for the convention, what places sounded good for lunch. We tugged at the scraps we had learned about each other through headsets. Surely, in five years on at least two nights a week at three hours or more each night, between our strategies for defeating computer-enemies of all different shapes and perils, we would have learned enough to produce something resembling actual human-interaction.

Fortunately, we had learned enough. But even through the good cheer it felt as if we were all afraid of letting the conversation break into silence like one massive blind date.

"How does it feel to be done with high school?" Rick, our other guild healer (and a real doctor by profession), asked me. Rick was old enough to be my father, and he kindly was letting Scott and I stay with him at the Hyatt.

"I can't wait for this summer to end so I can get to college already," I said. My smile slightly faded. I realized then that in a few months I would be seeing these guys less and less, until they disappeared from my life completely. Though most of my guild members were fifteen years older than me, I'd known them for practically a third of my life.

"What do you guys say we head on out of here?" Robert said.

"Let's rock," I said pushing the thought out of my head. I led the charge to the revolving door, into the blinding white light of the Los Angeles sun when I heard someone call my name.

"Hey *Ork*, Hertz is this way," Scott said. He waved us in his direction.

We followed him, clamored onto a bus, and then into our cars, and then we spilled out on to the LA thruway. We were Amy and Austin and Ben and Ed and Ellen and Ralph and Rick and Robert and Scott; we were students and doctors, scientists and salesmen, mechanics and bakers of cupcakes; we were dwarves and elves, gnomes and humans, warriors and priests and druids and mages; we were the guild *Disenchanted Enchantment*, named after a joke that we had all long forgotten; and the first dungeon we chose to raid since Grimlock's Lair the weekend before, the first dungeon we raided together in person: the Anaheim Convention Center.

There were entire species of geekdom I'd only ever thought were rumors. I learned that my guild was actually quite mild, but there: it did not matter. For as diverse as the nine of us were in our ages and occupations, there were thousands and thousands present each more distinct than the last. For every person like us that had abstained from coming in costume (though Austin had provided all of us matching shirts with our guild logo), there was someone that looked as if they had jumped straight out of the game. There were people garbed in construction-paper armor wielding foam swords, and people in boiled leather jerkins polishing forged spaulders. There were witch doctors beneath masks and hooded assassins, and there were elf women not quite as clad with leaf-covered corsets and armored bikinis.

As we waited for the convention center doors to open, we stood next to three guys, not much older than me: an orc, a troll, and a goblin -- our rival faction. Scott wasn't in line with us. I wondered where he had gone because he probably would have made some comment about our company. I usually had a retort, but only after Scott had made the opening remark.

Last night, after the nine of us had gotten our passes for the convention and returned from a Hibachi dinner, we had called it an early night for this morning. When Scott and I walked with Rick to his room, we opened the door to find only two queens.

"I could ask for a cot," Rick had offered.

"No, no, no. I'm fine on the floor," I said.

"Listen, I'm good if you're good," Scott said.

"Alright, if you say so," I said. And in case my face had reddened I added, "you want to be big spoon or little spoon?"

"You kidding? Look at me." He was twelve years older but a foot shorter. "I'm totally little spoon."

When I had woke the next morning, Scott was not in the room. Eventually, as we waited in line, Robert pointed at Scott waving at us from outside the guard-rails -- he had a pizza box in his hand. He called me over and handed me the pizza. I didn't want to look up to see if people were upset as Scott crawled over the rail.

"Thanks, *Ork*," Scott said. He took back the box and then dispensed the breakfast pizza to all of us guild members. Everyone besides Rick had forsaken *Ralph* and declared that I would forever be *Orkoth* or *Ork*. Maybe it had something to do with me being the youngest.

"Any of you scum want a slice?" Scott asked as he saw the orc eyeing the box of pizza.

The orc paused for a moment, caught off guard. Then he grunted, "I suppose we can call a truce -- just this once."

He reached for a piece and Scott snapped the box shut, nearly closing it on the kid's fingers. He laughed and said, "Can you believe an orc thought I was going to give him something?" He nudged me and I gave a small smile.

"Okay then," the orc said and turned looking forward. I heard him mutter *dick* under his breath.

"Scott, give them a piece," I said.

"What? I was just kidding," Scott re-opened the box but our rivals did not reach for a piece because the line had begun to move.

We certainly had underestimated the size of the line because the fog and the green lights spilling from the doors ahead had teased us much too long. As we drew close, all nine of us gave each other one last grinning look before we plunged inside.

"Ork, Ork, Ork -- look!" Scott tapped my chest with the back of his hand and pointed at a girl dressed as a purple-skinned elf. She had hopped over the gate of the closed pool area and was now dancing on the diving board. A security guard who had been monitoring this party on the tenth floor was at the fence yelling at her. She took a swig from the bottle in her hand and shouted, "Stay back! I'll bolt-lightning your face."

Her arm made the motion of hurling something, but she missed her footing, stepped into the air and fell to the side of the plank. Illuminated by the lights in the pool, tendrils of purple paint drifted from her body. The guard found the key to the gate, and he ran to the edge like a shark smelling clouds in the water. He grabbed the girl out by the arm and escorted her toward the exit.

"Good God, these people are crazy. I love it," Scott said sipping from his drink.

I nodded, and sipped from the beer that Scott had handed me. It tasted bitter. I didn't like it -- maybe if I'd been invited to those parties in high school. I brought it to my lips again and tried to drink it as long as I could, as I figured that come that fall I would need to learn to accept it.

We were quiet for a while. I tried to remember anything in Scott's life besides Robert or Amy. "How's Becca doing?" I asked. Becca had played with us a couple of years ago as a member of *Disenchanted Enchantment*. As far as I knew, she and Scott were still dating.

"She's good. Been busy. Says she misses you guys sometimes."

"Tell her we miss her right back."

"Sure," Scott said.

We stood against a wall with our drinks, and talked a bit about the convention earlier that day. We were excited about the new expansion that had been announced, and we agreed that the player-versus-player competition had some riveting matches. I saw someone on a balcony, a few floors above the pool quell the lights in their room with a tug at their curtain.

"I feel bad for anyone that picked this hotel for a little vacation this weekend," I said. Many of the ten-thousand that had excavated the convention center earlier that day had now commanded all twenty-floors of the Hyatt.

I don't think Scott heard me. He was pointing behind me, "There you go, *Ork*. At your six. You could totally get that girl from him." On a bench was a man with a witch-doctor mask flipped to the top of his head who was talking to a girl with gnome-green pigtails.

"Nah, I'm not going to get between them. They're talking," I said.

"Come on, go use those warrior skills to grab her attention."

"Maybe some other time." He headed in their direction. "Wait, Scott --"

"Hey, this is my buddy Ralph. He says he likes your hair!" Scott shouted, pointing his thumb at me. I looked at the ground and hid my eyes. Between my fingers I saw that she had looked up for a moment, and then returned to her conversation.

"That's okay!" He shouted again, spilling a bit of his drink. "He's not into gnomes anyway."

"Come on, Scott. Knock it off. Why don't we go back up to Robert and Amy's room?"

"Give me just a second, let me go talk to her for you."

"Scott, please."

"Alright, alright. I get it. This party sucked anyways."

We walked through the pool corridor and back into the labyrinthine hallway of hotel rooms. We tried to make our way to an elevator but I think that we were both lost. Eventually, I spotted a sign that gave us a directive arrow and we headed that way. When we passed through a lounge with a vending machine and an ice dispenser, we saw someone slumped in a cushioned chair. It was a girl with a single elf-ear made of cardboard, her other one nowhere to be seen. Her skin almost looked translucent. Then I realized that it was only splotched purple. It was the girl who had fallen into the pool. I looked around for the guard. He couldn't have just left her there. Scott was looking around as well.

"Hey lady, you okay?" Scott asked.

"I'm doing just good," she said, she raised her hand and fanned at us.

"Why don't you head back to your room," Scott said, placing his hand on her shoulder. "Do you have your key card?"

She emptied her purse on to the table. I sifted through the pile until I found the card. I handed the card to Scott.

"Room 704-E. One floor below our own," Scott said. "Come on, I'll help you there."

I collected the contents of the pile and scooped them back into her purse, then I helped Scott lift her to her feet. Her arm was still cold from the pool, and it felt like she had bumps where spots of the make-up had hardened. We only made it a few steps before she stumbled. She leaned on me and rested her forehead on my neck.

"You look like you play an elf like me," she said grabbing my nose.

"Do I now?" I said. "What's your elf's name?

"Lindy," she said, drawing it the name out an extra syllable.

"That's an interesting name for your character," I said.

"No, that's my name," she said giggling.

Even though I was holding her weight, I saw Scott hanging on to her hand and pulling her toward the elevator. We entered the elevator and he shifted her weight towards him.

"Alright, Lindy. We're almost there," Scott said. "*Ork*, before I forget, do you remember where our room is?" He shuffled Lindy on his shoulder like she were an infant, and pulled a card out of his pocket to hand to me.

"Yeah, of course," I said, taking the card. The doors opened behind me and I stepped out to give them room to exit. They lingered in the elevator.

"Alright, I'll meet you there in a second," Scott said. "I'm just going to take her to her room."

"Wait, aren't you coming along?" I said. Then I realized that we were on the eighth floor, our floor. "I can give you a hand. It's no big deal."

"It's okay, I can handle her. I don't want Rick thinking that I'm keeping you at the party."

"Rick, doesn't care --"

The doors closed before I could respond, and the elevator lowered to the seventh floor. I turned to walk back to the room. I didn't have to worry. I knew Scott. If I hadn't convinced my parents that I'd trusted these "strangers" then I wouldn't have travelled across the country to meet them. I had spent more time throwing myself at computer enemies and trying new strategies to tackle the next obstacle with members of my guild than I had spent in most of my high school classes. My guild and I: we would fail time after time, after time, until the one night, when all nine or ten of us had performed our roles as we had planned, that our enemy was finally felled. It was not the chance at upgrading our online-armor and fictional-weaponry that kept us coming back twice a week; it was the crackling sound of our headsets straining under the collective volume of ten cheers; and it was the need to see which scream belonged to every face that had made us all meet at the convention.

I turned back around.

I opened the door to the stairwell and descended to the floor below. I turned the corner to go down the Eastern wing, and then checked the halls that had extended from there until I saw Lindy hanging on the back of Scott as he fiddled with her door.

"Do we have the right room?" I asked. Scott slightly jumped.

"Jesus, *Ork*. You can't sneak up on me like that," Scott said. "I thought you knew where the room was."

"I did. I just figured that you might need a hand," I said. He scratched his beard and then looked at me. I couldn't tell if he was sober or not.

"You know, I'm beginning to think that we have the wrong room," he said. When the card refused to work yet again, he pounded his palm on the door. Then the hallway was silent. I think that Lindy had fallen asleep.

Suddenly, the echo of a chain being removed and the door-jam being clapped came from behind the door at 704-E. A woman with a phone at her head, in one hand, and a towel scrubbing the purple off her forehead, in the other, opened the door. When she saw us she hung up.

"Oh my god, Lindy!" she said.

"We found her sitting by a vending machine a few floors up. Luckily she had her keycard on her," Scott said as he handed Lindy off to the woman. "Do you got her?"

The woman held Lindy, and looked at Scott and I. She had missed a streak of makeup on her forehead and it made her brow look furrowed. She thanked us and then closed the door.

Behind the door, we heard a chain slide and a door-jam slap, and the hallway was quiet once more. Scott and I turned to go back to the room. He threw his arm around my shoulder.

"You know, *Ork*, everytime we drop a new bad guy, you always seem to get first dibs on the shield that drops." Definitely not sober. "But I love you, man. Us dwarves got to stick together." He stared at me with half-lidded eyes until I nodded and looked away.

We got back to the room to find Rick soundly snoring. I took out my contacts and brushed my teeth as Scott poured himself one last glass to drink, but by the time I'd gotten to the bed Scott was snoring, too.

I pushed Scott slightly further on to his side, then slid under the blankets. I wondered if we would be meeting per usual at our scheduled Dungeon-Raid next Wednesday, four days from then. If we weren't skipping the next week, what would we say when we did show up. Instead of trying to make progress on defeating Grimlock, we would probably just laugh about our trip in Anaheim as if it were already some fond memory. We would recall Ed's *In-N-Out* burger being plucked from his hands by a seagull, we would remember cheering on Austin and Ellen and Ben as they battled three other strangers in an online duel, and we would remember Amy secretly signing Robert up for the dance competition. But if Scott mentioned how funny it was when that girl fell into the pool, would I remind him that we had learned her name was Lindy?

THE FRANKFURTER
WILLIAM BEAN

F RANKLIN BURGENSON WAS AS ROUND AND WHITE as an egg, with a face as pockmarked with acne as a moon, and for a living he worked by himself at a hotdog stand in the city. His scalp glistened with sweat in the summer blaze as he handed another one to a small boy with black hair and a pasty face, wearing a black shirt with a UFO.

"Jesus Christ, mister, you're fuckin' fat."

Franklin frowned. "I have a thyroid condition."

"You smell like fuckin' shit, too."

"Just go away."

"What the hell didja do to end up with this job, anyways?"

Franklin's whole mass swelled like a puffer-fish, and his face blazed. "I'm... I'm older than you. I'll... tell your parents."

The boy cocked his head. "What are you gonna do? Eat me?"

Franklin's eye twitched. He rolled his sleeve, put on his best tough-face, which looked about as scary as a baby soiling its diaper. "You've... you've got another thing comin'..."

The boy took a bite from the hotdog, pretended to gag and spat on the side of the stand. "Your hotdogs taste like ass-wipe!" He hurled it, catching Franklin in his face, ketchup and mustard stinging his eyes. He rubbed his face on his sleeve, watched the boy run off. He trembled with anger.

If you asked Franklin how ironic he thought it was that he was kicked out of college for sexual misconduct, bailed out by his aunt, and now sold *frank*furters in central park, he would react in one of three ways: (a) his egg-shaped cheeks would swell and redden, (b) his beady eyes would narrow with rage, or (c) he would break down sobbing, depending on how much time had passed since his second lunch break. Fortunately, nobody ever had.

Franklin had always felt lonely in crowds. Thousands of people passed by his stand every afternoon to and from their offices and their workshops and their classrooms, and hundreds would bark and snap their fingers at him, wolf down their food and storm away. If they were not hungry or if they were on a diet, Franklin may as well not even exist. He handed out hotdog after hotdog with the numb efficiency of being no more than a bumper-sticker on the gigantic, churning machine of civilization.

He glanced at his watch. Five minutes until six. His shift was nearly over.

He'd sent out hundreds of applications to other universities, but no one would take him, not after the incident. He planned to go home and order enough KFC to polish off his piggybank and more than likely kill him with heart failure. If he didn't die, he'd go on a porn binge and put himself into cardiac arrest that way.

There was still three minutes left, but Franklin closed up anyways; he put away the sign, shut off the grill, locked the coolers.

"What, don't I get one?" said a woman's voice.

He ground his teeth. "Ma'am we're closed--" He looked up and his words trailed away.

She was tall, taller than him, but she was so gorgeous he nearly fell into an asthma attack. She wore red spaghetti straps over narrow shoulders, her skin pale and milky. Blond hair with orange highlights fell to her jeans. Her eyes were blue, large and pretty as pearls. He suddenly felt like a troll and wanted to hide back down under the counter.

Ruby lips puckered in disappointment. "That's too bad, I'll guess come back tomorrow then," she said.

THE NEW NEW ULTRA WEIRD

Franklin flung up his hands. "No, no! You, you can stay. Hold on a sec..." He bent down and rummaged through the cooler. "Let me just... start this grill back up real quick..." The grill clicked, the flame went up, and he fumbled around for another hotdog.

Finished, Franklin set the dog in a bun, squirted some ketchup, added relish, and handed it over.

"Thanks," she said, and then opened her mouth so wide her jaw appeared to unhinge, and with sudden ferocity tore off half of the hotdog, chewed it like a wolverine gnawing at a doe's corpse. The ketchup and relish dribbled down the side of her lips in the midst of her predatory chomping. Franklin gawked, unable to take his eyes away.

"For you they're free," he heard himself say.

She engulfed the rest of the hotdog in another bite, swallowed, and he saw it squeeze down her throat. She glanced up at him, her lips small again, and her eyes sparkled innocently. "Really? You're such a sweetheart! I'll take another dozen..."

Franklin dropped his tongs in shock. He picked them up again quickly, hoping she hadn't seen them hit the ground, and tore open another package of hotdogs. He didn't care if he stayed in central park frying hotdogs all night. In fact, he wanted to.

"It's so nice of you to do this for me," she said.

"Don't worry about it," he said, laughing nervously. "Do you have friends or something?"

She put a finger on her lips, batted her eyelashes sweetly. "No. Just me. I'm starving."

Franklin flipped the hotdogs and didn't ask. Whether or not a thin girl like her could eat a dozen hotdogs didn't matter to him; he just didn't want her to leave. He wanted desperately for her to speak to him again, but she sat patiently at the outdoor table, which was alluring enough already.

"Have I seen you before?" he blurted. "You look, uh... familiar." He lied, sort of. He wasn't even sure.

She tossed her hair, shrugged. "I'm a model. I was just on a Victoria's Secret commercial, had to wear this bra, that's where you probably saw me. I'm Izzy, by the way."

He felt his heart hurl itself against the walls of his rib-cage like a straight-jacketed madman in a padded cell. He was talking to a model. He'd finally scored. "Franklin. Uh… Burgenson," he stuttered.

"That's kind of funny. You're name's Frank and you're selling…"

He almost cringed. His cheeks started to burn and ripple, his fists started to clench around the tongs, but he looked at her face again. She didn't mean anything by it, he realized. He fell calm, continued flipping the hotdogs.

"I know it's ironic," he said. "Not sure how it happened. Wish it didn't. Wish I were still in school."

To his relief, she didn't ask, just smiled at him again, not witlessly, but with hope. Men must have murdered each other over her, Franklin had no doubt.

He finished the hotdogs, set them all sizzling in buns, put them all in little paper holders, and set them on the picnic table in two rows. "Thanks!" she shouted, and started grabbing and eating.

Franklin stumbled into a seat across from Izzy. She was going to eat them all. By herself.

He watched her until the sun started to set over the distant buildings surrounding the park. When she swallowed the last bite, Izzy belched with the force and volume of a jet engine, knocking Franklin over. She gently dabbed her lips with a napkin.

She got up from the picnic table, stretched, exhaling as she ran her palms down her own abdomen. There was just the slightest roll of flesh over her belt line. Franklin's mouth watered.

"Say, how well can you cook?" she asked. "If you don't mind me being too forward, I'd like to have you for dinner tonight."

Franklin wanted to ask how she could possibly think of eating after she'd downed a dozen hotdogs like it was trail mix, but he was much more afraid of saying anything stupid that would ruin the only opportunity he might ever receive in his lifetime to lose his virginity.

"I can fry up omelets like it's nobody's business," he said, pumping a fist and attempting much too hard to appear confident.

"Wonderful! I live in the apartment complex on 5th avenue, ninth floor. The door with the sunflower hanging on it. You're welcome anytime."

She walked away, her leather high-heels clipping the pavement. Franklin stared at her back, submitted to the urge to wet his lips.

Franklin did the truffle-shuffle down nine blocks back to his mother's house, stopped at the convenient store along the way and came back out with handfuls of condoms and lubricants. He argued with his mother, showered, rummaged through his wardrobe until he happened upon the only formal outfit he could find—a suit with a clip-on tie his father had given him four years ago. It was much too tight, but it had to do.

That night he came to the apartment, found the door with a knitted sunflower hanging from the door knob. He was dressed in a tie, his curly hair greased back, masticating three sticks of mint-flavored gum, and holding a bundle of rhododendrons in his hands. He knocked, squirmed nervously in front of the door.

The door opened. Izzy had changed into a black skirt, white blouse, and gold earrings flashed beside either side of her neck. "You're here! Oh, I love rhododendrons," she said, even though her eyes cruised over his entire body as she said so.

The dining room was minimal, but not threadbare. Vanilla incense burned on the table. "Why don't you want me to take you out to a restaurant for dinner?" he asked. Franklin surprised himself with how comfortable he was feeling around Izzy.

Izzy paused, what might have been uneasy. She seemed to think very carefully. "House dinners are more… personal."

Franklin shrugged. went over to her stove and refrigerator. "You said you wanted omelets? They're usually for breakfast, aren't they?"

Izzy brightened. "Who cares? Food is food, and you're looking great tonight by the way, honey. And hurry, I'm pretty hungry."

Franklin blushed, and he made himself busy rifling through egg cartons and knife draws. He chopped peppers, forcing his excited hands not to shake. Soon the room was filled with the scent of frying eggs.

"Have you ever, like… done competitions?" he asked.

She sighed, chewing on her finger. It may very well have been a dream of her's. "I can't. It wouldn't go over so well for a model's reputation if anybody saw one gorging herself."

"Uh... don't models have to diet?"

"Yeah, mine's is just... different."

Franklin flipped the first omelet. "You're not... what's it called? When you throw up everything?"

When she laughed, her voice was delighted, but her teeth glinted in a way that Franklin didn't altogether like. "Nope, not me. I've still got *all* my teeth."

"Did you swallow a tapeworm?"

"I'd considered that once," she said, "but now I'm on a very different... diet."

He flipped the omelets onto plates, brought them to the table. He went to grab forks, but turned to find that Izzy had taken to shoveling the food down with her hands.

"Uh... you don't say grace?" he asked.

When Izzy swallowed, Franklin watched again the contents expand and contract down her throat. "Grace," and she polished the plate with her tongue.

Franklin stared down at his plate. "You know, I'm not sure how hungry I am anymore," he said.

She took his plate, and the omelet vanished. "Thanks, honey."

He twiddled with his fork. "So... this, diet... how does it work?"

She stood from the table, went over to him. He could hear his heart thudding. She slid her arms around him, put her leg between his knees, and sat down on his thigh. She whispered, "Why don't I take into the other room and I'll *show* you how it works."

Franklin's head was spinning, with joy and terror. To think, he'd made plans to kill himself with KFC and pornography that night.

She pulled him into the bedroom by his tie. He felt a little like a slab of meat being carried down an assembly line. The door shut and locked with an audible click.

Before he could ask why she'd locked them in, Izzy pushed herself up against his large belly and guided him onto the mattress. She unbuttoned his shirt, threw it over the lamp. Every neuron in his brain exploded as her lips pushed his, lipstick smearing all over his face.

"I have to stay pretty," she said. "So I eat. It's magic, you see."

There was another click. Franklin blinked. He tried moving, but found his wrist handcuffed to the bedpost. "Wow, lady, I didn't think you were into that stuff--"

And then an excruciating pain from his neck. Blood ran into his eyes. He could hear himself screaming, his voice pitched into the highest octaves of delirium and agony. She reared back, loomed over him. Her mouth was full of his own dripping meat.

He begged, pleaded, but it was futile. Her jaws unhinged, and he vanished into the black abyss between her two ruby lips.

THE NEW NEW ULTRA WEIRD

TAR GOD
MARTIN BERNARD

E dward's Hyundai Sonata was a piece of shit. A blotch of rust in the shape of Africa plastered his driver's side door. His focus on the traffic was horrid. The day had been so terrible that he was broken down. He thought he might contract and succumb to some disease. A case of malaria was most likely brewing inside of his pasty white body.

He could not understand why she had gotten so furious. The Sonata came to a clunking halt at the red light. Consumer plazas sprawled endlessly in all four directions; Edward was occupying the absolute center. He realized why people refer to this country as an American wasteland: commercialism had stolen any possible priority to the aesthetically pleasing. It was a nation built for, and ruled by, men who strove to reduce all of reality to dollar signs. Edward imagined the Matrix for a moment, with raining cent symbols.

He had realized Beth was getting bored. He tried to be less predictable, but continuously gravitated to his routine mishaps. The bi-monthly over-withdrawals from his checking account, were complemented by a flow of letters regarding student loan default. The note she left was on the bottom of one:

June 12th 2014 - This is a reminder from
Sallie Mae. The default status of your loan sum

of 46,225 dollars is reaching it's sixth month. Please contact a Sallie Mae or third party loan counselor at your earliest convenience. January 12th 2015 is the final deadline.

Im Leaving. Im Sorry.

After a few more blocks of driving, Jake's duplexes came into view. The lawn's hedging looked less than amazing. The wood mulch was scarce, and had lost most of its burgundy color. The bushes had grown a foot outward into the lawn as if they were going to uproot and walk away..

Edward stared impatiently through the smudged windshield. Jake's front door was decorated with a cardboard shamrock, blooming from a beer mug. It was not St. Patrick's day. He had gathered evidence to explain why he did this. *Exhibit A,* was Jacob's upbringing in a suburb outside of Boston, an area of very proud irish ethnicity. This information is only useful in conjunction with Jake's obsession with *The Departed*, a Martin Scorsese film. Ed then multiplied these facts by the amount of residual bong resin in Jake's brain. That equated to the man who entered on passenger side, wafting a bouquet of beef jerky and Axe body spray.

"Your Shamrock is looking a little soggy," Edward had satisfied his need to bust Jake's balls.

"You have a cig?" Jake rustled through the cluttered center counsel as he asked.

"No, only black and milds."

"Oh... Trying to quit for Beth again?"

"Naw, she left."

"Again?"

"Again."

She must realize that I have all the time in the world to make things better. I am gainfully employed. Gieco is giving me a raise next week."

"Big boy money, now you can afford HBO.", Jake scoffed.

"Fuck off man."

The passenger hooked his ipod to the usb port on the stereo, and left the topic alone.

The cubicles buzzed with high school graduates selling affordable automotive insurance. Customers were delighted by the charm of that British lizard. This sent the masses flocking for collision coverage. They were more than willing to trust him in the event of a car accident. This always brought Edward back to those intersection thoughts.

"It's a bit creepy isn't it?", he asked.

Jake turned toward the question. He had to clear a mouthful of peanut M&Ms before he could answer.

"Eh wah cwapy?", He attempted talking through the candy instead.

"The idea of a cartoon character selling our customer's policies. I mean, it's illegal to do that for stuff that kills you, like cigarettes. So why is it legal to do it for insurance? Is that not just the other side of the same coin?"

"I don't know man. If I did, I would probably be teaching at a college," Jake was never akin to philosophical discussions.

"It's kind of like idol worship. You know? Like a secular idol."

"I think you just wish you were more important," Jake retorted. "Some people just have to work at Gieco man. Some people have to accept that their first girlfriend is not the person for them."

"All right..."

The car was a vessel of uneasy silence on the ride home. Jake was sincere in what he had said to Edward. This did not matter though. There was an unrecognized disconnect between the two friends. The driver of the car gripped on complete entitlement to his feelings. He was fully convinced that it wasn't matter of failed introspection on his part. The passenger felt justified insomuch as he knew exactly who he was. Jake identified simply as a guy that worked at Geico (*except for the weird Irish thing*). He felt that acceptance of the mundane created contentment. Jake also thought that Vishnu was something eaten with chopsticks.

Ed knew that Jake could not make his current living without his gracious shuttling. There was also the fact that he worked harder than Jake. That was his rock for the unjust nature of their equal monetary status. Trying harder than the other guy was a moot point. There had not been any passion in his own endeavors. Those that Ed knew who truly had, "earned it" stood vastly apart. Their dedication shined a spotlight on his half-assed college career. The pedestal he had just built turned itself on end into the mud. This was an impressive revelation for the distance between two street lights.

Edward was brought back to his senses by the flash of construction lights. He slammed on the brakes to keep the Sonata from kissing the back end of a cement mixer. The seized momentum threw Jake from the shoulders up.

"What the hell? You need to chill out and pay the fuck attention."

"Find a new fuckin ride to work then."

"Thats fine, bare with me for one more block. Then you can be the victim all by yourself."

"Quit implying that this is about me feeling sorry for myself."

"I meant accident victim." Jake was overly satisfied with his response.

"Get out of my— Jake left the vehicle before he could finish. Ed threw a hard fist at the center counsel, something cracked loudly. A cloud of cigarette ash plumed and began to settle on the floor. The Sonata made a sharp turn and cut out from the traffic lane. Ed slammed the brakes and scanned the sidewalks for his lost passenger. The Jake stood in the doorway of a bar and grill his back was to Ed.

"I'm not gonna bother," Ed grunted as he went to the glove box for some tissues. He wiped the ash and a little blood from his knuckles, then cursed at the sight of all the ash and butts on the floor.

The sound of jackhammers brought Ed's attention to the other side of the lot. The cement mixer he almost rear ended was now parked at a near by construction site. He realized the car was parked in a disgruntled fashion, partially covering three parking spots. An older woman, and presumable grandson, were spectators of Ed's sporadic behavior. They now had put considerable space between themselves and the Sonata. Ed made unnecessary eye contact which increased the woman's pace, with grandson in tote.

Embarrassed he made way to a Wal-Mart, and pretended he was an astronaut passing through airlock. There was always the first set of automatic doors. A rush of either heat or air conditioning providing the season, then another set of doors. That astronaut thought was more enjoyable now that he was miserable. There was a kind of hilarity in it then. He focused on the tops of his shoes as he walked by the greeter.

Ed was relieved by the direct route to the vacuum section. was return trip passed the deli. Ed's hand, still speckled with ashes, seized a box of popcorn chicken from under a heat lamp. The other firmly grasped the box of a Dirt Devil vacuum. Edward felt some strange triumph .

The ashtray was out of commission. Ed tried to put the broken halves together, a cigarette hung from his lips. Each time he daintily placed the shattered pieces into the dashboard compartment, they tumbled back to the floor. The construction hummed across the parking lot. Edward ate his chicken and watched. His legs planted wide out the open car door. The vacuum's instruction manual was twenty pages of nothingness. Edward read them over as a form of self-inflicted pain. He then realized that his bill was much higher than the vacuum's sale price suggested. A fist full of balled up receipts emerged from his coat pocket. He whined like a hound as tried to sort out the little mass of paper work. The back of his neck was become very heated and itchy.

The needed receipt emerged just in time for the wind to catch hold. A few flaps of its papery tail and it streamed out from his hand, across the parking lot. Ed mechanically stood up. He drove the heels of his feet into the pavement as he crossed the way. Each temper tantrum step stung his thighs on impact. He hoped that the earth could feel how nauseously upset he was. Meanwhile, one of the construction workers had moved to intervene.

"What'r you doing?"

"..." Ed was sweating profusely, and looked rather pale. He opened his mouth to say something, then closed it, then opened it again. The onlooker decided that lunch was more important, and cut the interaction short.

He felt wide awake in that horrible way. The kind of tight stinging awakeness that a person feels when they have succumbed completely to their stress. One foot clumsily stepped, then the other. Ed made his way to where the receipt had blown. The sound of a cement mixer grew louder and louder. He approached the abyss. (It was actually a hole about nine feet across that had been blown in the ground; the result of gas lines dating to the mid-60s.) Ed peered downward, finally realizing that he was in the grips of a panic attacks. His mouth let out another whimpering note.

He plunged forward into the hole. Tears streamed downward, the receipt at his feet. He had tripped, and fallen hard. His chin was cut on a piece of piping. It was bad. Blood streamed down his neck and staining his flannel.

The construction workers were distracted, and a lever had been pulled. The mixer roared and began to pour. Ed looked up just in time to kiss the liquid rock. He was being pushed hard to the earth. It was like fighting gravity, he crumpled under the weight. It was as if the weight of it all: Beth, work, failure, God, luck, and loneliness had finally just swallowed him up. In reality it was the concrete, followed by a fresh coat of tar to the road.

Things were pretty strange. At first there was a warm sensation that ran the length of Ed's spine. Then a piercing chill cut through the comfort, and his whole body trembled--twitches in every strand of every muscle. Edward felt like he had slept on top of gravel, underneath an elephant. The entirety of his body was asleep and tingly. Then, the first painful articulation of a limb. There was a recurring urge to just stand up and run, but every attempt was followed by hot lightning throughout his nerves. The most sound course of action was to just lay there and breathe.

There was the memory of coughing a lot. Edward sprawled out as best he could. Then, he spewed chunks of phlegm and stone. With each hacking cough he was able to clear more of the dense brown mucus.

After what felt like three days, Edward sat up, which was equivalent to — [STreTCHING aFTer SITTING In a CHUrCH PeW] X 10³ The atrophy of his lower back muscles scolded him for the sudden motion. He screamed. Then he felt amazing,euphorically so, until there was a rush of blood to his head, and he passed out.

He awoke in a bathtub, or something with all the sufficient conditions of a bathtub. There wasn't water--it was something else, thick and sticky, like molasses colored an opaque blue. Small mechanical devices swam like insects on the surface of the liquid. Frequently, one would crawl up onto Edward's skin. The first time this happened he tried swat it away. To his dismay, the blue goop was dense, and sudden movement was impossible. No matter how fiercely the man tried the goop could not be broken. He soon realized that the little mechanisms did not have mal intentions. They were each made of five jointed appendages connected to a central body. The ends of each mechanical digit was capped with some kind of sponge.

A few hours of struggling, and he had worked his way out of the tub. The sudden chill on his incubated skin caused sudden, uncontrollably, pissing. Edward ran helplessly in every which direction while the unending stream of urine panged against the metallic floor. He stopped, let his head fall back, and sighed. The light wasn't bothering him, his lids had swollen shut from exposure to air after so long. Instead of two ocular openings, there were two melted ping pong balls.

"Fuck." — He tried to rub them, jerking away his hands on contact. It hurt. bad.—

Feeling his way to a door, Ed slapped the walls as he inched forward. The back of his hand bumped some kind of console, and the door hummed upward. The swelling had receded enough to make out a faint image. A silhouette behind a large rectangular object.

"Hello Edward."

"Sup?"

"Well, your up Ed, you are awake. I hope the nap was long enough"

Colors and definition were returning to his eyes. Enough to see some grey, and the glint of gold.

"So I'm dead right."

"No, nothing like that. Too romantic. You have just been rejuvenated, you are a living fossil my friend. An example of a time much more confounded. You've been given a golden ticket of sorts. You are getting a chance to relive, retry, reinvent, who you are.

"Like in Super Mario?"

"What is a Super Mario?"

"Nevermind"

"I am going to be Frank with you Ed."

"Kay"

"The chance I am offering you is one of new beginnings. I am currently, in another lab, growing you a new...you. With all of the abilities you had wished for. You will be a savant, and athletic. You will have...flaxen locks, and washboard abs. You will be the recipient of unimaginable swooning. We will take all of your memories, your current knowledge, and conglomerate it with the psyche of your new self."

"Can I get a robe or something" At this statement the man at the desk coughed awkwardly. He hadn't seemed to notice the fact that he was eye level with Ed's genitalia until that moment. There were a few moments of silence. He sat. Ed giggled and shifted left and right on the cold floor. The man clapped. A door opened. Edward felt the weight of a fuzzy shawl fall onto his shoulders. He brought the apparell forward to conceal his frontal region.

"Better?"

"Kind of."

"Ed, this procedure will only work if you are willing to let it. A candidate must want this to happen or he will reject the mental transfer. That will cause brain death."

"I just want to go home"

"Are you sure?"

"Yes"

"Positive?"

"Yes."

"Okay"

It was as if someone had jumped a car battery, using Edward's head as a conductor. There was nothing but blue sky then, a nose bleed, a bathrobe, and a Walmart parking lot. Ed awoke feeling like he had washed down a gram of coke with a liter of Mr. Boston. He puked some more. Which felt like all he was doing as of late, puking. Ed got up from the pavement, still warm from the fresh coat of tar. He did a little spin, palms facing up and jiving, egging a universe aggregate of "*W.T.Fs*". The last option now, the only one that made sense, was to head in the direction of Beth's house.

THE NEW NEW ULTRA WEIRD

CLEANUP
CLARA TEE

M Y MOTHER TAUGHT ME to respect women, even though they might not respect me all the time; she taught me that women probably won't like the way I look and that I need to figure out a way to get past that. My mother was rude—but I respected her until the day she died (and all days after) because that's what I knew, and it's what I know.

If mother was alive, I'd be living with her. One of those "30-and-still-living-in-the-basement" kind of deals. Until last week, every time I looked at a woman, she looked away; how was I supposed to start a family when the only thing women see of me is my chubby exterior, adult acne, and slowly balding hair?

You see, somehow, things tend not to work out for me. I woke up the other day, and I felt different: powerful, strong. I got out of bed and committed to the normal routine: wake up, lay in bed for an hour or two, go upstairs and eat a couple bowls of Fruity Pebbles and watch FOX's version of the news until I have to go to work at Lapsus Memorial High School—janitorial. But after I finished watching the slander of Obamacare, I realized that the supply of Fruity Pebbles and other necessities (eggs, milk, microwaveable pizza) was running scarce, so I made the trip down the street to the grocery store and called in for the day.

I walked to the counter to buy food, but what I got was the first look I can remember a female giving me: it was the cashier. I walked up to her, boxes in my hand. She donated direct eye contact the whole time. I had seen her every three days for 5 years, and this was the first time she looked at me.

She was pretty. She was thin. She had red hair, like the inside of the top bun of a McDonald's burger, and she had white skin: onions, mayonnaise. I always wondered what her boyfriend was like. If he was fat and ugly, like me. She was young; she worked at this store when I first moved back in with my mother.

"Did you find everything you were looking for?" she asked. Her voice sounded like bacon sizzling, and her eyes looked like the burning grease. They were so beautiful; I knew she was only staring at me like one would at a derailed train. But the whole exchange seemed different, tense. Like something more could happen.

"Not quite, but it's alright." I'm not sure why I said that; I had my two-day supply looking me in the face, and I couldn't imagine what else in the world I could have wanted—except, in that moment, her.

That'll be $12.82. Credit or debit?" and nothing could have prepared me for what came next. As I handed her my card, our fingers touched—albeit, only for a brief moment, but that was enough. Upon connection, her entire physicality changed; her eyes, Kit-Kat brown, widened, and her mouth, Laffy Taffy pink, dropped open. She jumped on the counter, knocking over the rest of the week's food, and threw me down to the ground.

"Respect women," my mother used to tell me. "Respect women," she would repeat.

"What the fuck?" I yelled as I quickly threw Jessica, as her nametag declared, off of my body. She came back as quickly as an occupied hamster ball.

"Respect women," my mother would say. "Respect women," she'd repeat.

I was stuck. Jessica, the beautiful girl I had seen whenever hunger approached, was now mounting me at her job. This couldn't have been real. She clung on to my back with dull plastic nails. I tried

THE NEW NEW ULTRA WEIRD

to get her off. I had imagined this moment for quite some time, what it would be like to touch a woman, and all I could hear was:

"Respect women."

So finally, I got up the nerve to shrug her off of me. I stood up, and she fell. I ran out the door, but she chased me—and she was faster. This was too much romantic stimulus for me. I had never seen a vagina in person—let alone tried to inhabit one.

I tried to run down the street, but I hadn't worked out in a while (or ever). I started streaming sweat. It covered my face, and my eyes were blurry. Without being able to see anything, she jumped on my back, making noises that didn't sound human or alien, but animalistic in nature. And I, one final time, threw her off.

"Respect—"

The noises stopped. I looked down at the sidewalk behind me and saw her condiment-colored hair clumped up with ketchup. Her eyes closed. I thought I saw her breathe. I wasn't sure. Instead of looking, I ran away. I saw no cars on the street or people in my way. No one to see what I had done.

I walked back in my house, and my mother repeated herself in my head. I went to my mother's old room and sat at the left side of her mattress. I looked at the vanity dresser; photos were tacked into the frame of the mirror. One of my mother and I when she was alive. One of her parents, and my cousins, and I started to cry.

"Mother, I'm so sorry."

Of course, she didn't respond, but I had gotten used to that. She lay next to me on the bed; she had started to smell, but it wasn't severe yet, I told myself. I couldn't think of anything else to do with her. She was my mother. I couldn't disrespect her—by letting someone bury her in dirt or pick her apart like a toad on a stretcher.

"Respect women," I could almost hear her say. I had to listen.

THE NEW NEW ULTRA WEIRD

SPIT AND SWALLOW
FRANCIS IGUANA

H E ARRIVED LATE with energy drinks snuck in his backpack. Every eighth grader from Jason's class was at Brendon's graduation party, except Kathy the preteen tattletale. Jason met up with Brendon and showed him the contents of his bag, only to be trumped by the sight of four beer cans in Brendon's mossy knapsack. Gathering their usual troop, Jason threw his bag aside, and mobilized towards a narrow path far in the backyard.

The woods were fragrant with pine and kindling from bonfires along neighboring communities. Off the beaten path, the forest journey ended near a construction site with naked boards dormant in dried mud. Brendon jumped on the treads of a crane, sat down, and flipped open the flap to his bag. He pulled out the silver bullets and proceeded to crack his own. Landon checked his phone constantly, sipping and immediately making a sour expression after each swallow. Jason and Cameron took gulps ad talked about important things. What high school would be like, why it mattered who was still a virgin, and the trips they would take with flimsy licenses far away in time.

Landon's phone lit up with a punk song, *we are the fallen and we are the free*, prompting him to answer. Someone from the party was looking for Brendon, who proceeded to chug a half-full can at the sound of his name. He threw his empty can in front of the treads to be crushed and never seen three-dimensionally again. Cameron and Jason followed his lead and swallowed all of the fire, while Landon took a big gulp and gagged. Brendon took the can from him and muttered "Pussy."

Convening back to the mowed-down path, Cameron and Jason were still ready to explore. When Landon and Brendon were too far ahead, the pair saw their chance and cut into overgrown shrubs leading further into the swamp. Ground ate their new skater shoes like quicksand. The ire of mud turned bright white heels into an aged tan, while the boys laughed and pushed each other. Through one clearing, a picturesque pond appeared before the pair. The banks were steep and full of deep violet flowers. Cattails and reeds rose from tea colored water.

"Construction must've stopped here." Jason looked over at Cameron.

Cameron smiled, "Wow, yeah they fuckin' better have." The discovery of a hideout, a beautiful hideout at that, took the pair by surprise. There was a serenity before them, untapped and solemn in perpetual calm. Moments like these made adolescence that much more bearable.

"I kind of want to go in." Jason's shoes were already off, residual goo still ringed around his ankle. He took slow steps towards the murky chalice.

Cameron stayed back. "Have fun getting wet." He usually made tasteless jokes to entertain everyone, but by tiny laps of water and distant cardinal chirps he was demure and content. There was a strange absence of wind. Cameron felt relaxed, slouching against a pine's damp trunk.

Jason didn't care, he took off his shirt and shorts, running headlong towards the pond. Blades of grass felt like pockets of air beneath his feet. The setting sun and cool breeze created a loch of autumn in their suburban paradise. The water, motionless with

THE NEW NEW ULTRA WEIRD

smooth reflections, was beneath him now. Time seemed to stop, mid-air above the teacup. Jason curled into a cannonball and felt lukewarm water enshroud him. At the surface, his retinas stung, a malignant acid that felt like it was eating away at nerves.

"FUCK!" Jason yelled towards the shore. "This water is fucked up! Help!"

Cameron instantly stirred from his carefree lean and saw Jason blindly flailing in the pond's glowing center. The pond began to glow, an unnatural bright yellow, and something was inside it. A human-size fish was swimming circles around Jason's feet. Only the fish's black silhouette danced around in a pulsing glow. Each pulse grew brighter, until a beam as bright as the sun shot out from the waves, and blinded Cameron. The visionless boy stumbled towards the banks still.

The spinning current engulfed Jason, like a leaf stuck in a storm drain, screaming in bouts of terror. "Help me!" His eyelids were too heavy to lift, like rubber cement wadded up his tear ducts. The current churned faster, until its water became forceful to move against, and the fish brushed a leathery fin against Jason's bare leg. Moments after contact, Jason froze, feeling the fish slither around his sides. He heard something rise from the water, drips falling slowly, *one   two three.*

He was beneath the waves against his weakened will. A strange numb paralyzed Jason. He felt pressure pushing him deeper. His eyes flashed open, a gentle sting crept into his back, while a radiant light pierced his vision. Jason was delving still, he could swear he heard whispers, and beneath him a river of light swelled open from the pond's floor. The river flowed endlessly before him, shimmering like thousands of stars. The fish maneuvered in front of him, visible down to fine scales shining rainbows and the purest white he had ever seen. Above, there was a loud splash. As the fish swam through the river's light, Jason looked up, seeing enchanted colors of summer's bronze beneath the setting sun one last time.

The shore was empty where Jason awoke. Trees stood silent with arid heat trapped among their branches. Jason could see clear from his right eye, but the left throbbed with blurs that came in crimson hues. He remembered Cameron, the beer probably still settling in his stomach, and the blindness. Not a single living thing was there. Blinking, an uncomfortable sting came to the corner of his bad eye. He squeezed down, welling tears, and felt something pop out.

A small black mass fell to the ground, writhing around in freakish agony like a dying insect. The amoeba wriggled until steam rose from the pores of that slimy skin. Jason rubbed his eyes, and in that moment, the creature was gone.

Stepping out of the teapot, Jason stretched and found his clothes nearby. Under pearl moonlight, he made his way back towards Brendon's house. The absence of memories from murky waters left Jason wondering what'd just happened. He assumed the near-death experience caused him to hallucinate and see heaven's mythical tunnel of light. Jason stepped on the path, searching up and down for hints of downed grass.

Several minutes of searching yielded a path with short grass and few pockets of hungry mud. The suburban nomad centered himself by the familiar partition of trees. Up ahead a clearing parted with downed branches and leaves dangling still around their forgotten host. Jason emerged into the field. The wind grazed his leaking eyes, still flinching at sources of light. Brandon's backyard was devoid of the white tapestried tables and chattering adults previously littering the landscape. There was a pool where a lone green crabapple tree once stood. Jason stopped in his tracks, wondering if a wrong turn led him towards another neighborhood.

A balding blonde man, clearly not Brandon's red-haired Irish father, opened the wrought iron gate surrounding his dwelling. He shuffled out, letting it close behind him, and shouted over, "Can I help you?"

"Is this, am I at Brandon's..." Jason stopped mid-sentence. His voice seemed deeper. There was a heavy reverberation trailing through his vocal chords.

"You smokin' pot back there?" The man was approaching Jason. His face was a deceitful jolly, the smile Jason knew adults used when they wanted something.

Jason's eyes widened, "No, no, never."

"You seem pretty disorientated. You on drugs? Want me to call mommy? Hmm?" His stout figure plopped a safe five bodies from where Jason stood. He seemed pensive and wary at this distance.

"Is Cameron here?" Jason managed to respond, still hearing his own voice in a different tone.

The man stood his ground. "You've got the wrong house buddy."

There was no cell phone, wallet, or contents in Jason's turned out pockets. The clothes he wore were the same ragged articles as the day he dove into that pond. The fit of his cotton shirt was snug, while his muddy shoes nearly cut off blood flow to his feet. Jason wandered down Brandon's street, seeing new solar paneled streetlamps like alien heads glowing in the ethereal twilight. Down the street a patrol car picked him up, to which Jason had no misgivings.

He arrived at home ten minutes later, still the same home as he remembered. Little differences caught his eyes between glances from the escorting officers. There were new wind chimes with little golden birds fluttering along a wooden hut atop their tubular harmony. Neighbors watched the procession like guests at a doomed wedding.

Jason rang the doorbell. The officers looked at each other with confused smirks. Seconds later, Jason's mother cracked open the white door and her blue eyes met the weary gaze of her son. "Oh my god, what did you do?"

"I don't know!" Jason shouted, his body a vortex of shivers at the sight of his mother. She had aged into something different. The length of her feathery eyelashes had become engulfed by a pale ocean pooling beneath a frightened stare. She had gray hairs frolicking in the amber scalp that once radiated like pennies in the sun. Wrinkles gripped where her dimples used to well up as the officers motioned a hand towards Jason's chest.

"You don't know? Sure, I believe that, get your ass in here!" She grabbed Jason by the arm, her strength doubled since the last time she laid a hand on him, in the fifth grade.

Jason fell into the living room, breaking his fall against a puce couch. Another new item. The living room had lingering signs of familiarity. His great-grandfather's artwork remained hung in the same fashion along still white walls. A widescreen television sat where the old analog box used to be. The hallway light remained dim, thermostat adjacent beneath its sad little rays.

"Some guy on Fern Ave. called us about a kid whacked out on something near his house. We found him wandering down the same street, just looking around like a goddamn zombie." The swarthy officer to the left spoke with a condescending tone. "If it's any consolation, he's one of the most polite and courteous ones we've picked up."

"That's my boy alright, nothing but sunshine and bad habits." Jason's mother looked directly at him with a vicious stare.

"There's no need to worry ma'am, sorry to have bothered you." The officer turned around after he finished speaking.

The chubbier officer to the right nodded at Jason, "Stay out of trouble." And the door closed behind his broad navy shoulders.

The lock clicked with only a slight squeak, followed by a heavy sigh. Jason's mother looked towards him, only to turn her eyes away and place a veiny palm against her forehead. She was fighting back tears. Stale cigarettes mixed with a kiwi air freshener created some kind of foul oil scent lingering amid the tension.

"I'm sorry. I don't remember anything. I was hanging out with Cameron by this pond near Brandon's house and..." Jason stopped mid-sentence to see his mother's paralyzed expression.

Her pupils were dilated, streams of liquid had won against the valiant effort of her tear ducts. "Bullshit." She muttered, sniffling as she wiped away drops with her crimson sweater's arm.

"I don't remember anything! I was at this pond, I went to Brandon's house, but it wasn't Brandon's house." Jason paused to catch his breath. "I swear to God I don't know what happened, I don't even know where Cameron is."

"I don't believe you." Jason's mother had a harsh tone he was unfamiliar with. She spoke in it so eloquently like the words marched through her lips a dozen times before. She read into Jason's

THE NEW NEW ULTRA WEIRD

eyes, his body language, and none of it lined up. At this she shuddered and bit her lip, still moist with the cherry red of lipstick.

Jason, trance-like in his stare, tried to form a sentence. "I remember the pond that led to the guy who called the cops' house. Brandon didn't live there, but I swear that was the path I took!"

His mother quivered, the back of her fleece flowing like a tail. "What drug did you take? Mushrooms? Peyote? Did you go on some spiritual quest your stoner buddies talked you into?"

"I didn't take any drug! I was with Cameron and that's it!" Jason yelled now, his new voice striking nerves through every cell in his body.

"No you didn't." Jason's mother quieted herself. There was an unsteady calm about her, an analyzing stare deep into the strange of her offspring. Behind the brunette locks dangling over her pointed ears, a twitch sent one loose curl between her frozen stare. Moving her shaking hand to ensnare the rebel strand, she flipped it back in place, took a deep breath and spoke. "I know you didn't. I know you're lying. For fuck's sake Jason, Cameron has been dead for four years! What are you on?!"

The following day Jason refused to leave his room. Video game posters had been replaced by psychedelic pot leaves and Hustler models in pink lingerie. Not a piece of fabric escaped the stench of tobacco smoke and body odor. The bed he slept in had stains all along the squares of his mattress. His cell phone was the newest model covered by a dark blue plastic case. Throughout the day he got texts from names he didn't recognize with incomprehensible lingo and emoticons.

Following the argument with his mother, Jason learned that Cameron drowned in the same pond Jason lost his memory within. Cameron's body was recovered after a devastated Jason came running back to the party, barely able to speak in discernable sentences. Cameron's lungs were full to capacity when he was dragged out. His eyes were burned craters, the pH levels of the water were dangerously high and parasitic, which officers determined may have played a role in his death. Additionally, those who witnessed the excavation noted his pale smile. Cameron's face glistened with moisture and his cheeks bloomed rose along an eerie, accepting grin.

Jason finally saw a text he recognized. Brandon. The contact icon for him on Jason's phone was terrifying. Brandon's puffy cheeks were swelled to the size of baseballs, with a funnel gracefully supported by someone's cropped hand above his head. The red curls and freckles that dotted his cranium were replaced by acne and a flat buzz with the weakest hue of carmine. The backlit screen displayed *yo, down 2 blaze? baby is asleep.*

Outside, afternoon descended into a humid dark. The crescent moon barely etched into the frame of Jason's chipping teal windowpane. He hesitated as to what "blaze" meant for a moment. Jason developed habits he was previously unaware ran his life. Packs of Marlboro Reds strategically hid in crevices and dresser drawers like Easter eggs. Looking at them, Jason would salivate and want one without ever recalling an incident where he put a fragile sandy tan end of the cancer stick to his lips.

The other names in his phone must've all had a story behind them, and Jason figured Brandon would be the only sure fire way to find out. He tapped away on the glass screen, *sure, what's your address?*

Five minutes later, Brandon replied. *74 Edgerton. Lol u kno that.*

Jason emerged from his lair. The hallway was empty, his mother gone to work a night shift at the hospital. In the last few weeks before Jason lost his memory, she had been making fun of evening shift nurses, wanting to never become a night owl. She wouldn't converse with Jason since the night of his arrival. The front door was lighter, freshly painted a new shade of light red. Jason stepped outside, he had a driver's license, but no experience and no car.

When Jason first moved here in kindergarten, the street was a relatively new suburb. The black of asphalt leading up to each cement driveway was his tar monster. In faded blue overalls, Jason would find himself running up and slapping the hot street to tempt fate. Trees once stood in lots where playgrounds sprouted up with red iron springs and plastic slides. They were telling kids how to play now. The aging streets were so gray and lifeless, pot holes like acidic sores littered every couple feet.

Taking out his phone, Jason fired up MapApp, typing in the address Brandon gave him. A nicotine fit started eating away at his will. Looking down the right side of his strange old street, Jason moved in long strides. His legs felt like iron anchors. They were massive, sturdy as those damned trees. He must've been running more during the time he forgot. Jason always enjoyed track. Throughout the paralytic night before, he only took panicked gasps of breath. Tonight, Jason inhaled heavy tonics of oxygen and strode in quiet awe of the town he thought he knew.

The rosy brick house was much smaller than Brandon's previous abode. The garage door was open, piss yellow light emanating onto a driveway littered with gritty rocks. Jason felt the heavy crunch of pebbles popping beneath his sneakers. Brandon's dad still had his black and red striped truck. The tail permanently ripped off by an obese relative. Jason never tired of the story.

"S'up bro." Brandon's mass sat in a forest green fold-up chair. The same one his parents used at a little league game when they were young. He had gained weight, probably football, and all the beer. Behind Brandon, two clear tubs were full of icy blue beer cans. One pool overflowed into a dainty cat litter box by the right side.

"S'up." Jason humored him. Mirroring Brandon was what he used to do anyway. The memories of childhood were crystalized into Jason's mind. He felt immature, intimidated, and threatened to a degree. Time overran his mind, propelled him forward without a second thought. Jason raced through memories, anything to talk about with Brandon.

Brandon passed him an orange bong with white streaks that seemed to be dripping from the hole up top. "Hit this. You look like you need to chill."

For a split second Jason flinched. Peer pressure, D.A.R.E, all the classic tropes smashed into his judgment at once. Apparently he'd done this before though. Jason took the cold glass, used the lighter without thinking about it, and pressed his lips to the creamsicle. He inhaled the hit like the wind had been knocked out of him with a steel rod.

"Pull it out!" Brandon raised his voice.

Jason lifted the glass test tube from its resting place and continued inhaling. The sensation was hair-raising, his lungs felt sharp. Jason exhaled and caught his breath. "Wow."

"Some good shit man." Brandon took a hit and set the instrument next to his throne. "What's up with you man. You look scared."

"Just my memory man, I can't remember anything lately." Jason remained at a distance. He knew what happened may be believable, an extended kind of amnesia at best, but at the same time he had doubts on even friends taking him seriously.

Brandon's lips wrinkled, he seemed amused. "Smokin' too much man?"

"Probably doesn't help." Jason bemused awkwardly. The minor effects were kicking in, thoughts became slower, and anxiety rose higher. "Yeah, it's weird."

"What's like wrong exactly?" Brandon leant back, meaty calves spread like turkey legs, as his torso sank into the chair. This was the same loudmouth who called Landon a pussy just yesterday and now he was opening up.

Jason tilted his head down, "What have I been doing the past month?"

Brandon immediately answered, "You were acting kind of funny since last week. You got all sentimental and preachy. Then you wanted to go ham on just, life I guess."

"Go ham?" Jason bit his lip.

"We did that." Brandon pointed to the defeated mound of aluminum behind him. "You bought a carton on the reservation and told me you smoked half of it already. Got pretty baked every night of the week. Uhmmmmm, what else. You broke up with Courtney, oh, and you wanted to go back to that pond Cameron died in behind my old house. That was kind of, bizarre."

A tether in Jason's mind unhitched from the metal stake holding it firmly in his thoughts. The pond, he had never left the pond, Jason thought to himself. His thoughts became rapid, trying to imagine doing those things Brandon said. The same urge to smoke came back again, a slight jaw pain accompanied by salivating.

Brandon interrupted the thousand yard gaze Jason bore into his garage's stained beige floor. "I don't mean to prod, but I think your dad also set you off. The whole new trophy wife thing must be really weird."

Jason's mother had picked up her old smoking habit following the divorce two years ago. She resumed and Jason inherited. The divorce was one of many new surprises to Jason. His father had an affair and already remarried to his buxom mistress, Georgina. Go dad. The news reached Jason from Brandon, in all the juicy detail. He had a way with words, making the subtleties of Jason's personal torment sound like stand-up comedy. Jason thought of Cameron.

"What else happened? Tell me everything." Jason began grinding his teeth, feeling sandpaper texture where a chip appeared recently. He looked at Brandon intently, eyes curious like a raven.

For the next three hours, Brandon told Jason everything about high school. The beginning, Cameron's funeral, where Jason's aptly named rebellious side first appeared. What their friends did on the weekends and how most had obnoxious nicknames like "C-dog," "Diggles," and "Douchenozzle." Douchenozzle was Landon's pet name. Freshmen year Landon ceased contact with Jason, changing from his punk persona into a straight-laced, three season athlete with grades in the top ten percent of class. Jason dropped into the bottom rung of every subject, while Brandon had been expelled junior year for fighting a teacher. Brandon was engaged. They were together two years when he popped the question. She was four months pregnant and his parents were two years divorced. Now he was three years into the commitment, baby like a puppy, still bald and breathing in some adorable ball upstairs. Cradle adjacent to the blonde ponytail of a girl too sweet for Brandon. At least that's how he saw it. "But she's happy and dad's happy to have a granddaughter."

Jason had to come to grips with the life that passed him by. Not a single memory, a trigger, or detail could stir him from the confusion rattling through his mind. He lied to Brandon, "I think I have amnesia dude."

Brandon looked perplexed. "You don't remember anything?"

"I don't at all. I think I might've lost memories from that concussion by the lake." Jason lied.

"You've gotta be careful bro." Brandon went on to tell the story of how he got a career ending concussion junior year. A single blitz, headfirst he felt the force of a semi smacking brain tissue against the slippery ply of bone. He was a zombie for days. The head trauma didn't help the frequency of his already marked teacher disputes. Brandon said how he wasn't thinking properly. How it felt like he was someone else for the longest time. "I never wanted to lose myself like that again man."

Jason nodded, his skinny neck stuffed full of imaginary cotton balls. He wanted water, but his eyes kept grazing over the new Jason. The length of his tanned arms, more toned and muscular than before, stopped shaking. Jason saw himself in a broken mirror by the trash. His face slimmed down since middle school. There was the faintest vermillion shade of peach fuzz crawling down his cheeks towards a forming cleft. Damn genes. He looked at Brandon, smiling genuinely for the first time since he could remember. Upstairs, the baby started crying. Jason chuckled quietly, "I don't think it'll ever happen again."

The walk home was somber. A distant owl reverberated in trees across a shadowed grass field. The moon was half crescent, a bite taken out, like his mother used to say. Jason didn't know anything about himself or his loved ones. Flashes, sayings, and stories stuck with him like passages engraved in the way he navigated the streets. Brandon's eyes had met his with expectations, how to act, and what cliché to respond with when he cracked an inside joke. The lack of an identity, like the heartbreak of a relationship where one partner becomes such a part of the other, that they lose their way. Perhaps that could be his excuse.

His childhood street was a new wave of blue. The cool and darkened shade of ocean at night. The breeze grazed Jason's eyes. He blinked. Brandon commented how his eyes were different. They were the same shade of blue, like his mothers, but it was as if a pattern emerged. A cheetah print, with little black dots almost invisible unless you could look Jason in the eye like a lover, or at least Brandon who didn't bother giving anyone a comfortable amount of personal space.

After another bout of blinking, Jason rubbed his eye sockets. The porch light was on at his house. Bright like egg shells, and a gleam seemed to hang along the white paneling where shelves rose before ducking low again. The sun was nearing crest over the concrete length peering out from his driveway. His mother would be home soon, probably. Jason planned something magnificent to surprise her. To surprise everyone really. Entering the living room, Jason put his plan to work. He gathered all the cigarettes from his room and any pictures lingering of him with the mysterious Courtney. There was a golden picture frame with their faces pushed together and smiling as if they had won the lottery. He had found love for the first time, had lost his virginity, and he wouldn't remember a moment of it.

Gathering everything into a dismal pile, Jason sat on the couch cross-legged, and waited. The sun came up shortly thereafter and his mother pushed open the door. She was in pansy-coated scrubs and her face was a scowl. Looking up at her son, she was in awe momentarily, but immediately got pensive. "What're you doing up?" she looked at the floor, "And what's all this?"

Jason sprung from his position in tears. He welled all the emotion until this moment. The moment he first fell in love, he would never feel, the first touch of a girl. He wept uncontrollably and hugged his mother. "Mom, I miss her so much, I don't even feel myself anymore!"

She was dumbfounded. Her arms wrapped around the not-so-distant-anymore son like trembling rolls of dough. Pressing into him, she whispered, "It'll be ok, Jason, it'll be ok. I knew you were affectionate, but Jesus I thought you got this out like two weeks ago."

"I can't hide the pain. I don't know what I'm doing, I have nothing without her, and I don't know what I'm doing with my life!" Jason felt the words float out without a care. Without a wonder what the relationship could've been. He didn't even know her last name.

"I've been telling you that since two years ago. Goddamn it Jason, why now? Why not at the start of the year?" Her tone was sympathetic behind the painful smile.

Jason stopped crying and looked at her. This was every teenage boy's tragedy. He skipped right over the pain and into recovery. With genuine fear sweeping across his face like the sun creeping through the mildewed blinds before them, Jason just wiped away his tears, and said "I just don't know, I feel like a damn kid again."

Jason Yardley lost his memory for an unprecedented three years and eight months. He fully acknowledges that no matter what, those memories will not come back, and by forfeiting his high school identity Jason found his current memory to be more efficient and effective. He finished high school as a quiet observer, focusing on any test above social interaction. Seeing the sudden rise in grades his senior year, Cameron's parents donated a year's worth of tuition to their son's old best friend as a surprise scholarship during the graduation ceremony. The remainder of his college fund went to charity, though talk of Cameron during their speech got emotional for everyone who knew the fallen classmate. Days after, Jason spent the rest of summer telling stories about Cameron still clear as glass to his parents. The attention to detail was picturesque, and as Cameron's mother said, "It's like it was all just yesterday."

In the coming fall's crimson hue, Jason went to Henderson Community College. No subject in mind, just a fresh start, and an openness to new things. His mother detested Jason's previous lack of will to apply at a college with dorms and only at the last second decide on community college. In truth, she encouraged it to free up her home for private dates, but her son's newest attitude was warmly welcomed. Henderson was small. A handful of liberal arts students and a pretty big pre-med population. The buildings were all tan brick complexes with diamond squares around the sidewalk. Silver clam laptops sat on the slender bellies of phantom black hipsters every day. Jason was intrepid in this new realm, making new friends with ease in each bright and different corridor. He ran with life, neck and neck with every passing moment, winging it. Living in the moment.

Brandon remained Jason's closest friend. Missy, his daughter, would be two this year and the wedding would approach shortly after. Jason would be the best man. Both still smoked weed together, Jason claiming it helped with the depression and amnesia. Though the past remained a sobering void, Jason longed to try and relearn the truth of what happened. One summer night, when cicadas cried out in their harmonic lulls, Brandon and Jason returned to the pond. Though Jason didn't reveal his intentions, nor did Brandon know the truth, they found the hazy lagoon once more. Jason stepped into cool water, careful not to submerge his eyes in the herbal poison. He felt a fish swim by him once more. Scales grated across his leg, texture like a wet rake. He did not fall under this time. Instead, the fish circled Jason for hours, creating a golden glowing current that circled and hugged him with the warmth of an old friend.

THE NEW NEW ULTRA WEIRD

WHERE THE WILD THINGS AREN'T

JASON J. JONES

Alfred Green lived in a hole in the woods.

He crouched over a pile of twigs, banged two rocks together until his fingers bloodied. A spark jumped, sizzled in the brush, and a wispy tongue of smoke trailed up to the ray of sun bleeding in from the vent above. He blew into the debris until a beautiful red flame kissed his moss-tangled beard. He tightened the deer-skin around his shoulders.

A worm wriggled from the dirt wall. He pinched it between his fingers and pulled out its slimy length, raised the worm to his pursed lips. "Forgive me, my wild brother," he whispered. "Let each part of your body nourish me, and may your spirit be reunited with Mother Earth." He slurped it up like a string of spaghetti. There was his dinner.

He had had a full day. He had awoken in the morning, crawled out from his burrow, and a mellow fog hovered in the hollows among the pines. He had hoped down the bank and drunk deeply from the creek. Finished, he raised his head and spotted a family of raccoons huddled up in the branches of a tree, cowering from a boy with a slingshot. Alfred had promptly lunged from the brush nearby and pounced on him. Later, he stumbled upon a rabbit, choking in a noose. Quickly he'd untied and freed the creature, then taken back to his burrow, and now he nursed to health. Its furry body shivered in Alfred's lap. He stroked it, and named it Henry David Thoreau.

His eyes fell back on the fire. It was his only warmth for the night. He cringed. By keeping himself warm, he was invariably emitting dangerous carbon dioxide gases into the Earth's precious atmosphere. "Forgive me, Mother Gaia," he said. For ever since man had discovered the power of fire tens of thousands of years ago, it was also an engine of pure evil and destruction.

Alfred abhorred the entire human race. It was a virus, a cancer spreading across the face of the earth, multiplying, sucking up the planet's resources until nothing was left. Hairless apes, beasts, and monsters, all of them! It was as if the entirety of human history was a collective effort to annihilate all that is green, living, and fecund. Even the ones who half-heartedly wished to save this planet were despicable to him.

Alfred made endless efforts to rid this planet of their existence.

Or at least make their lives hopelessly inconvenient.

A week ago, he had snuck into a backyard shed and stole a box of nails, and he scattered these nails across the interstate on a regular basis. He snuck into a construction site and jammed the lever in the backhoe. Yesterday he sabotaged a hunter's tree stand by sawing a hole in the fabric seat. All in a day's work for the guardian of the Earth!

There was only one occasion in which Alfred could be sighted outside of his wilderness home and in the metal thickets of civilization. Once every month he attended the committee meetings, where he pronounced his litany of petitions: Tear down the power plant! Disband the logging company! Give the squirrels the right to privately own trees as property! It ended the same every time, with the entire committee voting unanimously against his cases. Alfred bared his teeth in a chimp's grin, stormed out of the courthouse in a rage.

He approached a parking meter, sniffed, and raised his leg to mark his territory. Across the street, two police officers walked out of a coffee shop, one tall and pale and the other potbellied. The fat one glanced over, dropped his donut. He tapped the tall one on his shoulder, who turned, and his jaw dropped. As the tall one whipped out his radio, Alfred bounded into an alley.

Crossing the parking lot, he kicked a Lexus and its alarm started blaring. What a disgraceful species which he had the biological misfortune of being a member! Why wasn't he born a raccoon, or a majestic elk, or an imperious bear? He could spread a rabies epidemic, or maul hunters. He scowled at the rising buildings, the crooked sidewalk, the cars and trucks endlessly belching and roaring their noxious fumes. If only he wielded the power, he would demolish every single accursed edifice in the city, grind up the flesh of every human and sprinkle it across the land. Their flesh would nourish the new trees and feed the animals that would reconquer the lands it had lost.

He passed through Central Park. What a tiny, miserable excuse for a natural environment, like trying to impress a woman with fake roses. The benches, the fountains, the ugly little gazebo were all bitter disillusionment that, even though these trees grew tall and proud, they would be suffocated eternally by the bustle and the pollution of a human habitat. Alfred snorted and tugged at his trailing, mud-caked beard.

His steps faltered.

Before him stood the most beautiful tree he had ever seen! A birch, imperious and elegant, its papery bark casting a silver sheen in the glorious sun, towered over him with a sheltering spirit. Its branches arched over him, like a mother's welcoming embrace. Alfred treaded up to the trunk, his knees quaking with reverence. He raised his hand, set his palm upon it. It was thick, strong, and smooth, like a temple's column running up to the blue arch of the sky. How could this arboreal majesty sprout up in the middle of this despicable habitat?

His gaze lingered down the length of the trunk, until he notices a point close to the grass, where two branches spread open curvaceously, revealing a dark, narrow cleft with brown lips. Slowly, he glanced over his shoulder.

Across the lawn, an old woman sat on a bench, scattering bread crumbs to a flock of pigeons. They pecked and warbled. Alfred's whiskers twitched. She was probably poisoning the pigeons, no doubt.

He turned back to the birch, drew his fingers over the soft mossy lips of its orifice, shuddered. He whispered sweet nothings into a small knot that passed for an ear, stroking the silky bark with the back of his fingers. Beneath his deerskin robes, his tick-infested member quivered and bloomed, like a budding branch filling up with thawing spring sap. Alfred brought his belly up against the tree, pressed himself until he could feel each fiber drawing up the life force from the bark. His phallus peeked out, exposed in the air. His whole body trembled.

His ear quivered at a nearby sound.

A radio emitted fuzzy static, followed by electronic gibberish ("*Cchhttzz!* Officer Warren to Officer Brad, I specifically ordered angel cream, dammit, it's coming off your pay, over— *Ccchhttzz!*).

Alfred craned his neck around. The two police officers patrolled the turf. The fat one hitched up belt, yawned. The tall one glared across the park, spearing every blade of grass and flower with his gaze with suspicion.

He turned. The woman on the bench by now was staring fixedly at him. The bag of bread slipped from her hands, spilled on the sidewalk. The pigeons wandered over and pecked frenziedly.

He tucked his member away, slipped off the tree, and scurried away.

Alfred Green never committed the act of coitus with a human woman. With mankind's population exploding out of control, would not be a heinous crime against the Earth to populate it with yet more parasitic chimps? And for what? The sake of satisfying his own primitive urges?

He ran after the does over the hills and meadows. He approached the swans with melodious serenades of honking and squawking, and his sharp squirrel's cry was practiced and refined to wooing perfection. Once, Alfred had fallen in love with a lady raccoon. How dark and sleek her fur had been! Together, they had terrorized countless camping families and plundered endless marshmallows and Hershey's bars. Then one day, he found her at a dumpster, dead. She had choked on a bottle cap.

But as for this birch tree, he had never felt such a degree of passion. Her name, he knew he'd heard her whisper, was Sophira. She was the Mother Earth incarnate, silent and watchful guardian. He crawled back into his hole and filled the forest with his bitter, wracking sobs.

He lit a fire, cradled Henry David Thoreau in his hands, but even the silent company of his rabbit no longer aided his spirit. Now that he had seen such beauty, he could not live without it. And humanity, damn them all, would stop at nothing to drive him away from her. He closed his eyes, whimpering, and then snoring.

In his dream, he was in a garden that spanned the universe.

He found himself treading through a colonnade of titan redwoods. Gazing upwards, he was overwhelmed by the canopy cradling the heavens. He started as a flock of birds scattered from branches, beating wings and singing. He lifted his foot curiously from the grass, where under his feet lilies, orchids, and roses spread across the grass in a vibrant, living mosaic. Motes of light danced over pools of crystalline water, while dragonflies zipped and skipped across its refractive surface.

As he tread, his heart singing, glowing leaves whispered secrets with every soft push of the fragrant breezes. Sweet pollen wafted into his nostrils. He snorted merrily, and began leaping over the grasses, fashioning himself after a gazelle.

From all around, and from an infinite distance, came the cool rush of running streams and a chorus of ten million frogs, birds, and bees all warbling, peeping, and droning. The wilderness moved past him, yet it was as if he traveled no distance through the impossible Olympian wilderness. This would be the new earth, he thought, if only he could find a way.

Somehow, after minutes or eons of footsteps, he entered the center of this new Eden. Sophira his tree ruled from a throne of serpentine vines woven into filigrees. As he drew near the tree, its branches rustled and its trunk twisted, like a majestic lady turning her shoulders from her view over a balcony. The silver bark flashed in the sunshine. Alfred's heart raced as the trunk morphed, its knots and creases bending until it resolved into the shape of a heavenly female face.

"This world grows old, Alfred," she said, bark-lips shaping to the sounds, a pair of eyes like flaring emeralds. "I need you to renew the land, to make what was wrong now right."

Alfred collapsed to his knees. His desire was unbearable. It broke out of the cage of his soul.

The mother-tree continued, unfazed by this man's exubrious exultations. "I charge you with a sacred task of purification. Your seed will prevail!"

This world vanished into blackness. He stood in the void. The weight of oblivion crushed him ten billion times over.

Ululating with a chieftain's sorrow, his hands ripped the fungus and hair from his head, pounded his chest with fury.

He awoke, jabbering and sweating. The fire was a pile of ashes.

As the beauty and horror of his dream receded into the subterranean parts of forgetfulness, a reality made itself evident. He did not want to accept it, but unless he did, these dreams of Sophira would continue to torment him forever—even after his body decomposed in soil and his spirit flowed in the harmonies of the universe.

He had to go back to the city.

Dusk painted the sky ochre as he climbed over the fence. It was not beautiful. It was the ozone layer, burning away every minute like a flame creeping across a precious fabric, blackening and curling up along its path.

It was Sunday. Police patrol had eased down. As long as Alfred stayed off of the main streets, he had little fear of being caught again. The revulsion of simply treading near these monstrous, brick parodies of natural habitat was enough to make him stave off a perpetual, crippling nausea.

When he found the birch tree, it had no beautiful face, but as Alfred came under its spreading branches, he felt the hair on his back bristle with the sacred vibrations of its ephemeral beauty. The sun vanished behind the forest of buildings. Shadows retreated into the darkening night.

"Why do you provide your shelter for them?" he whispered, squatting low and bracing himself. "They do not deserve your grace."

The tree did not speak. But he did not need it too. The whispering breeze among its branches was all he wished.

So he began with his love-making. It was like soaring over the earth, and under him was all of creation. In less than a minute, he thrust his hardest and felt the spray of his seed filling the deep cavity. Something inside hissed, and suddenly there was sharp pain as of a small rodent burying its teeth into his member. He ripped himself out, howling. A gray squirrel scurried out, its coat sticky and shivering. It chattered bitterly and crawled down the trunk.

Alfred retreated back into the forest. He tore up long aloe leaves and used them as bandages, wrapping them gingerly around his punctured penis. The juices stung worse than a swarm of hornets, but that was for its healing properties cleansing the injured reproductive region. The bleeding, at least, had ceased.

Arriving at his burrow, he came across a sign posted to a lean hickory tree. PRIVATE PROPERTY. He tore it from the staples in the bark, crumpled it up, and ate it. Then he crawled into his burrow.

To his further dismay, Henry David Thoreau was gone. It was cold in his den, and his loins ached too badly to gather any kindling. So he curled up in a muddy corner, hid his face, and wept. "Sophira," he thought, "why have you betrayed me?"

When the year passed into autumn, Alfred began to gorge himself on all the nuts and tubers he could scrounge up for the coming winter. The dreams of Sophira passed, yet until the first flakes of snow danced down to the pine beds, he wondered at her mysterious will—after beckoning him through his dreams, why would she so suddenly scorn him?

Biologically, no ordinary human could ever survive the brutal winters of any deciduous region. To Alfred, that is what made them so pathetic and unworthy of existence. For he had learned from a wise old black bear the simple technique of hibernation. How to shut his eyes and never open them, how to release his mind from his frozen body, how to will the beating of his heart to slow down to the pace of a dirge. It was so simple, staying warm—because once you realize you are already warm, not even the harshest blizzard can crystallize your cells. But humans are not simple. That is why they could never survive on the planet which raised them.

It was in the midst of hibernation that he dreamed of Sophira again.

He sat, cross-legged, under her swaying boughs. It was painfully silent in this forest which seemed to inhabit the rift between dimensions, while his heart was screaming.

"Why do you scorn me?" Alfred begged.

"Our time together was finished."

"But I wish to be with you. Forever."

Hesitation, long enough for a thousand new species to evolve and die out. Finally: "I know."

Alfred stood, outstretched his hands in a lover's indignation. "So why humiliate me? Why drive me away? What do you want with me, O sacred spirit?"

Her leaves were perfectly, vibrantly green. They crept down low and brought him in an embrace. Her voice, or else it was just the branches shifting, said: "For I feared for your safety."

The tree assuaged his fears and heartache with the delicate tenderness of clouds brushing against a mountain, each vapor of sympathy perfectly soothing his feverish thoughts.

"If you stayed," continued Sophira, "they would have found you, and imprisoned you in their dungeons of mortar and dread."

"So by hating me, you loved me?"

"I only ever loved you."

Alfred burst into tears. How foolish, how errant he had been these last moons! To think that such a perfect creature of Nature would ever be so cruel, it was something like heresy, only far, far worse.

"I am sorry," Alfred moaned. "Sorry!" He crashed to his knees. He wished to dig a hole in the enchanted grass and bury himself. "I believed you something you are not. What shall I do to earn thy forgiveness."

The bark-features of this glorious birch tree shifted to a stern expression. "Only come back to me," said the voice of ten million butterfly wings. "For now the time has come. Awaken!"

When he opened his eyes, it was spring. Winter had never passed in such a seemingly-instantaneous fashion since Alfred retreated this wild abode.

Immediately, he understood the message of Sophira. He scrambled out of his den, stretched. He looked down, saw that all of the fat he had stored for winter had burned in the midst of his dreaming, and now he was as thin and lean as a young wolf pup. The sun basked his skin.

He crossed the interstate, several back yards, and loped his way into the town. No one would be searching for him—it had been months since he'd attempted to mark his territory so foolishly. Now he could almost hear audibly the voice of Sophira calling to him. As he passed a convenient store, a flower shop, and a cheap motel, it grew louder and louder, until his heart wished to burst out from his mouth and flutter away.

In Central Park, the grasses were filled with dandelions. A town worker in a ripped up hoodie was weed-wacking at the roots of his precious birch tree. Alfred approached him, seized the weed-wacker, bent it, and hurled it across the lawn.

"Hey man, what gives?"

But with one flash of his teeth, the man shrugged his shoulders and lumbered off to the truck for a sandwich.

He returned his amorous gaze upon the birch tree. "Oh, how I missed you during those cold winter months..."

Then he noticed something very strange, blinked. Above the cavity between the two large spreading branches, the trunk was swollen. It appeared as if the tree had engulfed a beach ball, bulging forward and leaning the tree forward. A small knot on the surface of the swell gave it the undeniable appearance of a belly button.

Curious, he raised a hand slowly, reached out to touch it.

There was a moan—or else it was the creak of the trunk bending, one could hardly tell—and he quickly flinched back. Whatever thrived dormant inside the tree was moving. The swollen part of the tree convulsed, then contracted, convulsed, and contracted. It emitted another low sound, irrefutably with a tone of laboring agony.

He stepped back. There was something *inside* of the tree.

The birch tree groaned again. The object trapped inside the trunk pushed its way downward, moving down slowly like an esophagus. The tree made a small, high-pitched noise, as painful as branches snapping. It huffed and puffed. The only way Alfred could describe it was *greeching.*

He hurried to the foot of the tree, for some reason found himself instinctually cupping his hands below the cavity. The creaking, groaning, and greeching grew louder. Its branches kicked terribly, shredding apart its leaves. Alfred peered up inside the shadowed cavity. Indeed, there *was* something inside. It was alive and staring back at him.

He jumped back. The tree emitted its loudest greech, heaved one last time, and the thing inside of it projected out of the tree's cavity. It spilled in the grass with a wet "plop!"

He crawled close to it, sniffing cautiously.

The thing was shaped like a fetus, but made of a soft, grey whorled wood. It was slimed-over in sap. A vine sprouting from its belly hung from the tree's cavity like an umbilical cord. It's folded limbs had just begun to make weak, infantile movements. A single leaf budded from the top of its melon-sized head.

He picked it up in his hands. Sap ran between his fingers. The infant's lids cracked open, revealing walnuts for eyes. The mouth opened like a nut-cracker's and released a cry as soft and brittle as twigs and leaves crunching underfoot.

He cradled his child in his hands. Suddenly, he was all the more grateful. For this child was a gift from Nature, the one true mother of all. In a vision, his future projected in his mind's eye. He would take this creature back, raise it as his own. He would come back to Sophira, again and again and again, and raise many more. They would be a nation together, a new race that would bring Nature back from this dark age.

It all started with Alfred's seed.

THE NEW NEW ULTRA WEIRD

THE ALIENS WHO RUINED EVERYTHING

BARRY BAXTER

RAY COOPER WAS KNOWN as the greatest science fiction writer of his time. Hugos, Nebulas, and Locus Awards cluttered every corner of each of his eight mansions. Magazines would have published his grocery list if they could have gotten their hands on it. And now, at the very height of his fame, he had just signed a contract with the SciFi channel—they were producing a mini-series based on his novel about an alien princess who led a secret life as a space pirate.

Then real aliens made contact with the Earth.

~

When it happened, Cooper was signing books at the mall, after a long conference about the ridiculously enormous success and the revolutionary scope of his latest book. He barely remembered the title of it, and frequently needed to glance at the megalithic displays flanking his chestnut table in the lobby. Now he found himself scribbling signatures into books, shaking hands and making small talk with people he instinctively despised, for over six hours, and he felt as if the marrow in his wrist bones had been cauterized with a laser beam. He glance up as he handed a signed book back to a fan, only to discover that the line still snaked out of the door. It made him realize there was an uncomfortable constriction in his bladder, and within seconds, he realized he had the perfect momentary diversion.

Cooper stood up abruptly. "Using the bathroom, everyone." He waved them off dismissively. Several security thugs pushed against the seething crowd as he retreated into the lavatory.

He pissed. Nothing else had caused him to come so close to an orgasm in months. Whilst urinating, Cooper slipped a notepad from his pocket and wrote a novelette about a Plutonian man who discovered his wife was cheating on him and so blew up Neptune over it, zipped his fly and flushed.

At the sink, he splashed his face with cold water. He couldn't take another day of this publicity. People had always evoked his anger and irritation, but in his dreams of being a book writer, he had never anticipated having to deal with them on this grandiose scale. If only this cold water could freeze him, store him in a cryogenic hibernation until a distant age in the future, one in which humans were nothing but old wives tales for whatever new species dominated the planet. He would tear open a portal to a parallel universe where he had never been born, or had at least decided to never publish a book. Or with the royalties he made from writing his books, buy a private rocket and launch himself to another planet. Just anywhere, as long as he could write indefinitely, and there weren't any humans.

He'd attempted to write in at least three psyudonyms, each one exposed. He was baffled by his own misery. To be a famous author, this was what he had dreamed of since he started composing haikus with crayons on napkins when he was a toddler. It seemed nearly unfeasible, completely pathetic, that now he had the author's dream he'd want to push it all back. He could hardly stand his own whining, and yet he knew he must be the most miserable man on the planet. Why couldn't he simply be happy?

Cooper did not believe in God, and he never will. His request was directed at the universe itself, to any omnipotent powers who may or may not have been listening.

"I don't want my fame anymore," he muttered. "Just take it all away from me."

Cooper emerged from the lavatory and strolled back to the table, making a frivolous attempt to be amiable to all of his adoring fans. He was very confused, however, when he realized that everyone in the lobby had forgotten of his existence. Every head was fixed in the direction of the television. Cooper turned his attention to the television, too.

The television hanging in the small parlor cut to static. The florescent lights flickered. Cell phones lost WiFi, 3G networks were rendered useless. An awful murmur swept through the room. A dark murmur swept through the snaking line of fans. The manager flicked through the channels, but all were static.

The static on the television jumped to a screen filled news banners shouting BREAKING NEWS and EMERGENCY ALERT and LIVE FOOTAGE, because a flying saucer had apparently just landed in Washington. The world watched as a shiny chrome disk, aflash with bulbs and antennae, glided past the Washington Monument and hovered over the turf. It extended tripod legs and gently touched down on the grass.

Shock quickly seized hold. Someone dropped a copy of his book. An old woman in a babushka flopped onto the floor and foamed at the mouth. Some people ran out of the store. Others clasped their hands over their ears and started gibbering. While others simple stood and stared, jaws agape at the revelation that they were not, in fact, the only sentient life form in the universe. But Cooper, rubbing his aching arm, just stared at the screen. *Jesus, this looks like something out of the* Twilight Zone, he thought. Cooper slapped his forehead. So goddamn cheesy.

Within twenty seconds, the army had the flying saucer encompassed by an absurdly large brigade of armored jeeps and tanks, guns bristling directly at the thing. The spacecraft rested on the turf like a gigantic bug. Eerie silence followed.

The trap door in the saucer began to open, steam rushing out, the hiss of hydraulic peraphanalia. Predictably, the trigger-happy humans fired every single gun within one mile at once, engulfing the flying saucer in a maelstrom of flames and debris. The television screen flashed blindingly. Cooper, watching, figured the United

States military was unleashing virtually every weapon in its stockpile short of nuclear warheads.

And, just as predictably, when the dust settled, this barrage of ultimate human might left not one dent on the polished chrome surface of the alien spaceship. The trap door continued to descend, unfazed, until it touched the grass. Cameras peered closer and focused on the shadowed opening. The anchor was rambling on off-camera somewhere about this being the most momentous moment in human history... something or other. All Cooper could think was that if Joseph Gordon-Levitt walked out of that thing in a spacesuit, he was going to shoot himself.

The aliens emerged. Three transparent amoebas, boogers as big as Buicks, and uglier, slathered out from the cockpit of the flying saucer. The army opened fire again, but bullets and tank rounds simply rebounded from their gelatin masses. The blobs simply proceeded forward, oozing ahead with gelatinous determination.

The screen suddenly went to color-tone.

As the chaos died in around him and people began to regain their wits. He did not sign a single other book that night. He was glad about that.

~

Ray did not believe in aliens.

Don't get the wrong picture. For being heralded by the Times Magazine as the greatest science fiction writer of the 21st century—which to him was a presumptuous and even laughable title—Ray was a chief skeptic. Nobody save a backwoods birthed, incestuously bred creationist could deny the overwhelming odds of the existence of sentient life somewhere else in the universe. For Ray, whatever intelligence vast, cool, and unsympathetic that was watching the human race as we bustled along our day-to-day tasks, if it were truly intelligent, it wouldn't bother to contact us at all. Perhaps study us like lab rats with the occasional abduction, maybe even a secret meeting with every new President, just to pop in and see if we've gotten anywhere yet. But a wise race of aliens would do best to stray as many light years away from Earth as possible.

He saw the Earth for what it was, a hopeless ball of mud flying through space, populated by a species of semi-evolved apes that have contrived every fashion of dooming themselves and making mundane, everyday life absolutely miserable. The future, for Ray, held nothing but doom. Nuclear proliferation. Global climate change. Political upheaval. Economic disaster. And iPhones. Nothing came closer to the effects of a memory-wiping laser, in Ray's opinion, as a game of Angry Birds. That is why he wrote science fiction.

And this is why, after the incident in the bookstore, he canceled the rest of his tour and locked himself in his New England mansion for three months straight.

His agent called. Ray snatched up the phone and blurted:

"I already told you, Houston—no more tours." Yes, his agent's name was Houston.

"On the contrary, it doesn't look like you could go on another tour even if you decided to," he said. "Ray, you're not doing too well. You dropped off the Best-Seller list two weeks ago. As a matter of fact, if you let me be honest, nobody's bought a single copy of any of your books since the Amoebians arrived in March."

Oh Houston, superfluous as always. "... Who the fuck?"

"God, the *Amoebians*! The aliens! That's what people are calling them. You're my only client who doesn't own a television, you know that?"

Ray twiddled his pencil in his fingers, pretending it was a mothership sailing through the void of space. "It's a hoax. Leave it to the federal government to fall back on every single science fiction cliché to stage an alien invasion."

"I wish it were that easy," said his agent. "But the market trends over the past few months show a completely different story. Since the contact, sales in books, DVDs, Netflix, all of its tripled! Mostly romance, fantasy, murder mysteries. It's just... science fiction that's down in the dumps."

"Can you provide a diagnostic report, Houston?"

"Simple: escapism. These are scary and confusing times, especially with the Amoebians restructuring our civilization, and lots of people really don't want to face it. They've even banished KFC.

People want a place they can go where things are clearer—bright colors, wine and food, good and evil, none of the post-modernism of the last thirty years."

"Science fiction is *the* escapist genre."

"Ray, your books are more notorious than H. G. Wells or George Orwell for being ominously bleak about the nature of people. I let my grandson read your last manuscript and now he's taking medication."

"All right. What the hell are you saying?"

He heard his agent cough discreetly over the line. "Why don't you write a fantasy book instead?" she said.

Ray resisted the urge to hang up the phone. Barely. "Excuse me?"

"Just look at George Martin. He used to be writing sci-fi, and now—"

"It's *science fiction*. Please, there is a very distinct difference."

"Sorry. He was writing science fiction, and then as soon as *A Song of Ice and Fire* came out, bam! That's all anyone knows him for. It's a shame, in a way, but you've got face the facts."

"He betrayed us," said Ray, clenching the pencil, and it snapped in his hand. "I'm not going to whore my talents to another genre—if you can call it one—just to appease the masses. You know my golden rule. I write for myself first."

Ray harbored a bitter hatred of fantasy, nearly maniacal. It was the sell-out of speculative fiction. Science fiction? That required comprehensive thought and logic, a skeleton of solid fact to support the robust, beautiful flesh of the conceptual. There is no magic. Nothing ever *is* just because it *is.* Not unless you were dealing with a woman.

"These aliens are giving science fiction a bad name," said Harold, "as if it hadn't already been on the decline before they showed up."

"I'll think about it," said Ray.

He hung up the phone. Houston's failure to understand the occupation of writing as art rather than business always struck a raw nerve in Ray's near-translucent temper. But he hadn't sought a new agent. After all, Ray had a new rule, to keep himself from becoming totally isolated and at risk of killing himself—as long as he could tolerate a person more than his ex-wife, he knew he should still remain in contact with that individual.

Ray hardly scribbled another word when the phone rang again. Fuming and muttering, he glanced the caller ID. Bob, his producer from the Sci Fi Channel. Begrudgingly, he whipped the phone into his hand.

"We're canceling the production of your script," he said.

"What?!" His fingers squeezed the phone. "I signed a contract. Doesn't that count for anything?"

"We just can't run your show anymore," said Bob. "It's not just you, either. We've got to cancel shows left and right, up and down, even side to side. Our ratings are plummeting fast. In fact, we've got to sell the entire network."

Now Ray was genuinely aghast. "What is wrong with science fiction?"

Bob replied with partiality. After all, no matter what disastrous forecast was predicted for the media industry, he was guaranteed to retire with enough money to purchase Nigeria and turn it into an amusement park. "We took a poll recently among a couple thousand of our viewers. They just aren't going to buy into aliens anymore, not when everybody knows what the real aliens are like these days, and the real aliens, to be frank, well... they suck. They say science fiction is a dead genre."

"This is an outrage," Cooper blurted. "What about *2001 A Space Odyssey*, or *1984*? These science fiction stories are way past their expiration dates, yet people still love them! Who do you think you are?!"

The producer hung up on him.

Ray hurled the phone out a window. He looked back at his book. He wrote, hesitated, and then found himself rifling idly through the unbound pages. Reading over his own words, he was beginning to feel extremely stupid. For nearly forty years, he'd taken his stories and the stories of countless others as seriously as religion, built a career and a literary empire with his imagination. Now it was all so suddenly absurd.

Contrary to his agent's chiding, Ray did own a television, which was enclosed in a cabinet in the living room. He turned it on to the news. He lit a cigarette, and for the first time in a year, set himself down onto a sofa with the grace of a skinned shark flopped onto the deck.

The blobs were escorted to the White House. The Amoebians understood that we humans were merely puny, semi-evolved apes, incapable of preserving ourselves from extinction. So they assisted the human race by overseeing an effort toward world peace— disbanded militaries, stabilized economies, and abolished every religion by proving the true origins of the human race once and for all. The universe and all sentient life within it, they proclaimed, was simply a projection of their omnipotent imaginations.

Meanwhile, Cooper sat on the sofa, staring numbly at his ashtray, struggling with his own existential crisis with far more civility than the rest of his species. The question of the existence of life elsewhere in the universe had now been answered, and now it had afflicted Ray with the most severe case of writer's block he'd ever had in his life— the only one, in fact. Since humanity was about to be enlightened as to its origin and its destiny, what was the point of writing anymore? If the Amoebians were here to stay, he realized, then he could never write again.

~

"I'm leaving."

His wife was agonizingly beautiful. She was also very sad and very angry, which somehow made her even more beautiful, like a flaming meteor hurtling towards the Earth. Two suitcases sat on either side of her. Their son, small and quiet, nestled into her long skirt. It was scorching in his study, but he'd been in a very bad mood, since his wife was leaving after all, and so when he was in a bad mood he wrote stories, which was virtually all of the time.

"You love sitting at that desk more than you love us," she said, as if she hadn't been saying it for years already.

Ray did not look directly at his wife, but at his son. He'd lost the custody battle over him. He was small and pale and blue-eyed, just like himself. Intelligent, but his mother would quickly dampen it with her incompetence, he figured.

"I just can't get through to you, can I?" she said.

Ray winced. His eyes lingered to the window. Birds twittered.

"I only have one thing left to say to you, Ray. I no matter what, I still love I'a sothogrum illif'git uuumba ghhrraaaaggh."

Ray looked back at his wife. Her face melted into a translucent ooze, absorbing her dress, the suitcases, and their son.

"Blurg blub glub bub reeeghiz—please report to the town hall, citizen," a clear voice very much like the voice which would often speak his own thoughts said, "where we shall all unite together to direct the course of humanity's bright future!"

~

Ray awoke. The Amoebians had interrupted his dream for a telepathic broadcast, most likely, if his judgment of conventional science fiction tropes were correct. Whatever the case, he did not report to the town hall the next day.

He puttered around his house that morning, found himself actually considering his agent's suggestion. He'd never gone twenty-four hours without writing, and it was becoming debilitating. That was it. He would try to write a fantasy book.

In the moments he crossed the room and logged into his computer, Ray had already composed the first several chapters in his brain. Instead of writing, however, he puttered some more with desktop icons and checked his email.

He nearly missed a message with the subject heading, "House Foreclosure." Ray clicked it.

It was not a house foreclosure notice.

Dear Author,

The future of our Earth and all stories is at stake. If you are concerned even a single iota for the future of all science fiction writers, please do not report to the Amoebian town conference for which you have been telepathically summoned. We have reason to believe that the Amoebians have malevolent motives behind their so-called "charity."

These infernal blob creatures, by their mere existence, seek to destroy what is most valuable to humans as a species—our stories. There will be a congregation of all members of the Science Fiction Writers of America and the Directors Guild in my studio hangar to decide the next course of action to take against these enemies of narrative. Please join the resistance.

Yours, with all the Power of the Force,

George Lucas

PS: To avoid detection by the alien occupiers, this message will now self-destruct.

Remarkable. A personal invitation from George Lucas. He wasn't usually this obtuse, though perhaps the man's voice was different in his letters. The hairs on his arms and neck prickled. As he read the final line, Ray heard his computer tower suddenly heat up and emit a clattering noise as if a ferret had just had its tail chopped off inside the thing. Instinctively, Ray dove from his chair, in time to avoid an explosion and a barrage of fragmented motherboard and plastic. His computer was destroyed, yet Ray wasn't a tad bit angered—he'd just been emailed by one of the god-emperors of science fiction itself.

Ray packed a suitcase hastily. The Amoebians would be expecting Ray at the town plaza. Having written several dozen books based around conspiracy theories concerning aliens, Ray already knew what to expect—the Amoebians likely sought to brainwash the human race, starting in small towns and working their way to greater cities, in the next phase of their diabolical takeover. Ray paused with his underwear in hand. That, or they might be revealing some more secrets about the universe for our enlightenment. For a minute, Ray was tempted, but to see George Lucas, his childhood icon, in the flesh and speak to him, well... that would be far more enlightening than anything these half-evolved blobs could bestow upon him.

He left his mansion wearing glasses and a fake mustache and a trench coat, a disguise from any fans he could have come across in town, and a tinfoil hat to protect his head from the telepathy rays the

Amoebians were likely using to monitor every human being on the planet.

Arranging for a flight was, of course, an ordeal itself, what with the new traffic of flying saucers constantly patrolling the skies. Ray glanced out the window. He could not even find respite from the alien threat in the beautiful view of a panoramic landscape; the countryside was scattered with crop circles. He could have sworn he spotted one with coencentric circles and said SHOP AT TARGET.

The plane landed in Los Angeles. Ray left the airport and took a taxi, donned once again in his human/alien disguise. The palms of Hollywood swayed in the breeze. Pedestrians strolled along the sweeping boardwalks. The waves crashed on the white shores of in the distance. It seemed nature paid little mind to the alien invasion.

Ray arrived at the video production studio. A man stood at the door.

"Hey, no blobs," he said. "We need a retinal scan first."

Ray was flustered, gestured at his body. "What the hell? Do I look anything like one of the aliens?"

The man shrugged. "Sorry, Mr. Cooper, but there's a rumor that these aliens can shape shift." He pulled out a gun-looking metal pointer-scanner-thing. "Here's a GLMPST. Lucas himself bought these. Not even an Amoebian can fool these things." The guard scanned Ray's eyeballs and allowed him into the building. One stood outside, while the other guided Ray down several corridors and down several flights of stairs. At the deepest level, they came to a gargantuan titanium sealed door. Cooper never would have guessed that George Lucas had actually installed gigantic titanium sealed doors in the deepest levels of his video production studio, but of course, he had eccentricities like every artist. The guard scanned his hand, and the door opened with a monolithic clatter and sweeping lights on its surface.

Ray Cooper entered a room that was an identical replica of the Jedi council safe room—a small, circular chamber with several windows separated by metal pillars and overlooking an electronically-generated cityscape of the Republic metropolis. There were the twelve seats, all occupied save for one of them, and as he took in this breathtaking scene, he recognized every occupant of this grand chairs: Robert Silverberg, Gene Wolfe, Ursula Le Guin, Octavia Butler, Max Brooks, Orson Scott Card, Ridley Scott (who was projecting himself via a hologram), Ted Chiang, and C. J. Cherryh. Ray was only one microscopic unit of common sense away from completely believing in an afterlife and believing he had just entered it. A childish giddiness he had not felt for several decades nearly made him say that this could have been the Justice League of Science Fiction.

"Samuel Delany," Ray muttered under his breath, aghast. "I'm honored. I've read all of your books."

Samuel rose to his feet, as round and jolly as an African-American Santa Claus, and shook his hand heartily.

The theme of the empire began to strike its ominous tones from hidden speakers in the vaulted ceiling. The door to the chamber opened, and all eyes turned.

George Lucas strode into the chamber, earth-toned Jedi robes billowing, light sabers clasped to the hilt of his belt. He appraised the members of the council with a casual sort of modesty that really contradicted, in Ray's opinion, the grandiloquent scene he had set in place. Such was a director's role, he supposed,.

"Oh good!" said Lucas, "I see everyone responded to my email. I was hoping I didn't sound too melodramatic about it, but you really have to take these things seriously, you know?" Lucas turned his mild-mannered gaze to Ray. "That chair on the end is yours, Ray. Put on this robe and have a seat."

He threw Ray his own Jedi's robe. Ray put it on and he set himself down beside Samuel Delany, staring at George Lucas the entire time, hoping that the carbon dioxide of his breath might filter into his own lungs and carry his genius with them. It felt so good to be among these people, because in a way, like him, they weren't really people at all, but living, breathing story-engines.

Lucas stood at the very center of the elaborate circular embroidery on the floor, and addressed the council. "I have gathered you all here today because there has been a really, really big problem for anything related to science fiction in today's world—since these aliens arrived on Earth, it seems nobody appreciates what we create for them anymore, not our stories and not our films. There can be no doubt that this is a part of the alien's schemes, to make the human race forget what's most important to us—our stories.

"So does anybody have any suggestions?"

Ridley Scott immediately chimed in, his holographic image flickering and voice fuzzed over a little. "Well what's clear is that people think that science fiction is irrelevant, now that we have all the answers. These aliens just made all of my face-huggers and Engineers completely moot. Now that we've all seen the actual Engineers of the human race, who's going to still take mine seriously when I finally finish my sequel to *Prometheus*? No one, apparently. I can't see a single reason for the form of these aliens supported by evolution. My aliens could beat these blobs in every department; xenomorphs that reproduce via face-hugging phallus-vagina monsters is much more thrilling than these Amoebians. Right?" There were grumbles and nods of affirmation all around.

"Without science fiction, no one will think about the future anymore," said Robert Silverberg, fingering his silver mustache. "I wrote a short story, called 'When We Went to See the End of the World.' Time traveling is a business, like a travel agency, and anyone can book a trip to the point in time when the world ends. But whenever the characters go see the end of the world, each one has a different experience." Ray wished he had thought of the idea. "Everyone has their own vision of the future. Science fiction opens the imagination, and while perhaps a science fiction story will never predict the future, we can all have the freedom to develop a vision for ourselves. Science fiction has a bad reputation for attempting to predict the future, and usually being wrong, but that isn't its purpose: science fiction inspires the future. The Amoebians will take that freedom away from us if we don't stop them!"

"The real problem," said Ted Chiang, "is that our audience wants either a story that is based in our real world or a story that is complete bullshit—I mean, fantasy. My stories are neither. They aren't even plausible. 'Hell is the Absence of God,' my thought-experiment in a world where angels and demons empirically exist, isn't supposed to be real—it's supposed to be *true*. Not true to reality, but true to human nature. People falsely believe that science fiction is about answering questions, when it's really about asking them. I've never attempted to prove the existence of God or the justification for either worshipping him or not with that story, but I wondered what world would look like only if it all were actually real—would things really be any different? I don't think human nature changes a bit."

"If you ask me, it is human nature to avoid a crisis until it's too late." Max Brookes brandished a shovel in his hands instead of a lightsaber, eyes darting in case of a zombie outbreak. "If no one has been asking twice about the motives of the aliens, they won't even when they're shipping us all back to their home planet to bake us in their pies. True, these aliens aren't humans, but I think the problems they're causing us are actually the same problems we seem to experience on our own world. I wrote about zombies, sure, but it wasn't all just about zombies—I wanted to demonstrate the incompetence of governments in the face of a disaster, and people in general; just take a look at New Orleans. Everyone knew the levies weren't going to hold, but did we do anything about it? Science fiction was on the decline even before the Amoebians came. Now these aliens seem to just be emphasizing that problem on a bigger scale."

"Let's not forget the family unit as well," Orson Scott Card said. "In all my novels, I create characters with a stable family consisting of a mother and a father. When the family unit is disrupted, such as in *Ender's Game* when Ender is taken from his family by the military, it is traumatizing. The world needs science fiction, because it speaks out on social issues in a way that other genres don't—by literalizing that issue in a fictional, hypothetical world. George Orwell did that with *1984*, by writing about a totalitarian regime in the future, and I think we can all agree that, while it didn't predict the future, it inspired people to avoid such that kind of terrible future. As for today, there's the homosexual revolution. The homosexuals are destroying our democracy, and if we don't do something, the Amoebians are going to destroy the sanctity of marriage! They're changing the constitution when we need to keep these rules in the books—"

"And just who do you think you are, Mr. Card?"

Shadows and a fearful silence settled over the chamber. Samuel Delany had arisen from his seat, eyes locked in indignation in Orson Scott Card's direction. Cooper had no idea the man was even capable of anger, yet now he quaked in fear. "Science fiction has no room for agendas," he boomed. "It is anti-authoritarian. It is not gendered; though most typically view it as a masculine genre. It defies categorization. I will not tolerate the likes of such as you, Orson Scott Card, to ruin the free spirit of science fiction!"

They lunged from their seats. Card whipped out a beam gun. Delany pulled out a ion-axe. They closed in towards each other.

"Enough!" George Lucas stepped between them. He flashed his lightsaber, and it hummed in the air. "Something's coming!"

There was a loud boom from outside the chamber.

Silence. Heads turned. A panicked murmur swept through the room.

There was more banging reverberating from the extensive pipework in the ceiling. Clearly, something was making its way behind the walls.

"Jedi," said George Lucas, "stand ready!"

Vents burst open, and the Amoebians flooded into the room. George Lucas spun about the room, cutting down blob and after blob, and then he leapt into the air and performed a spectacular flip, slicing an Amoebian in half, and landed dexterously on the other side of the room.

Ray's arm was nearly sucked off its socket, and he turned to find himself engulfed by an Amoebian. His efforts to break free were futile. He was quickly sucked into the gelatinous form, and then could no longer breathe. The world grew dark. Dark as his hope left for the human race.

~

Ray awoke on a steel table, his wrists bound spread-eagle, a blinding ethereal light searing his eyes. As his pupils dilated and the light subsided, he discerned the shapes of three Amoebians looming over him. *Great*, Ray thought. *I've just been abducted.*

One of them stretched their mass out into an appendage, wielding a very large purple crystal scalpel towards the spot between his eyes.

How are you holding that? said Ray.

HUH? it telepathed.

I mean, you're essentially a liquid, right? So how are you holding that scalpel? Why doesn't it just fall through your body and impale me?

DO NOT DISRUPT THE OPERATION, the Amoebian replied to the other, who was becoming very confused and irritated. ALL WE NEED IS TO ACCESS HIS IMAGINATIVE FACULTIES AND REMOVE THEM. THEN THIS PEST SHALL BE ERADICATED.

That's really going to bother me.

YES, WE HOPE IT WILL BE PAINFUL. WE'RE IN A BAD MOOD BECAUSE OF YOU.

I'm talking about my question you never answered.

SILENCE! YOUR ECCENTRICITY HAS INTERFERED WITH OUR ACTIVITIES ON YOUR PLANET it said, choosing to continue to speak in a voice loud and booming and monotonous enough to make all-caps necessary. But no longer.

I know why you hate science fiction stories.

The scalpel halted, suspended a hair's breadth from his forehead. AND WHAT IS YOUR HYPOTHESIS, PUNY HUMAN?

Anything a human being can imagine is better than what you aliens really are; cheesy, trop-ish, boring, cliché, and completely void of all creativity.

THE HUMAN SUGGESTS WE ENVY ITS IMAGINATIVE FACULTY, IT SAID, SEETHING WITH ARROGANCE. It and its alien henchman laughed, which telepathically is very loud and very painful to the hearer, WHEN IT ONLY INHIBITS A LIFE THAT WOULD BE MUCH MORE PRODUCT WITH REALISM AND LOGIC, SUCH AS WE HAVE ATTAINED. WE ONLY WISH THE SAME FOR THE HUMAN RACE.

You would destroy imagination!

THE REASON FOR YOUR FAILURE TO ASSIMILATE INTO HUMAN SOCIETY HAS NOTHING TO DO WITH YOUR PUNY IMAGINATIVE FACULTY IN YOUR BRAIN. YOU

CANNOT TOLERATE HUMANS, BEFRIEND THEM OR COPULATE WITH THEM, BECAUSE YOU YOURSELF ARE NOT HUMAN.

You lie! My father was a heroin-addict! He gave me a copy of War of the Worlds before he killed himself.

NO, RAY COOPER.

I AM YOUR FATHER.

Rage consumed Ray, at the lie his entire life had become, so much that it gave him the strength to break his bonds. He pulled out the lightsaber that the aliens had oh-so conveniently left in his belt and cut the Amoebians to pieces.

The alarms sounded. Ray dashed through the corridors of the ship. Each author, he discovered, had been individually imprisoned in the same fashion as himself, and he freed each one in turn.

The crowd of disheveled writers dashed toward the exit when, to the left, a squadron of Amoebians came oozing from an offshoot corridor. All the doors in the ship were closing.

"Max!" Ray called out. "Prop the door with your shovel!"

"I don't have it," he cried. "I left it behind!"

"I have this situation under control, my friends!" Samuel Delany barged ahead, trampled his way toward the shutting exit door. Relentlessly, he heaved himself under the door and pressed his shoulders against it. Between his strength and his girth, his strength barred the door.

"What the hell, Delany?" Max Brookes cried. "You broke one of the most important rules of my *Zombie Survival Guide*—don't be the hero!"

The writers bustled under the door, passing Delany who stood like Atlas as laser beams from the Amoebians fired aimlessly in all directions except their targets. Ray Cooper was the last to depart, and he turned back to Delany. "Please, you have to come with us!"

"I cannot," said Delany. The spaceship was exploding behind him. Amoebians were scurrying about, with absolutely no idea how to fix their smoldering ship that they had destroyed in their own rage. "I mean, I really can't—" Delany's body gave way and the door threw him to the ground and cut him in half. Even at the brink of death, he managed to flash his whimsical half-smile, as if he had found some deep truth that nobody else figured out yet, but that's okay, just give 'em time, once they're as old as you are they'll finally get it. Then he died.

A tear ran down Ray's eye. He examined it curiously. It appeared Samuel Delany had bestowed Ray with the gift of sympathy. How had he ever written a single story without it?

Ray Cooper walked out from the space ship, which had, throughout the course of their escape, crashed onto the street of a city. To his amazement, more of the Amoebian spaceships had teetered out of control and collided into skyscrapers and plazas.

He wandered toward one of these ships, which had landed in a coffee shop, and found one of the Amoebian pilots crawling out from the wreckage. It was quivering, writhing, and rasping and sneezing. There was no need to ponder the reason why all these aliens were suddenly being poisoned from Earth's atmosphere: the common cold. What a shame. Good thing the Amoebians had never read H. G. Wells, or else they may have avoided such a simple, stupid error and been successful in conquering the human race. The blob fizzled up, leaving only the sticky residue of slime on the broken shrapnel of its space ship.

He rolled his eyes, went inside and ordered a double-espresso.

CONFABULATION

THE NEW NEW ULTRA WEIRD
A HEATED DEBATE

This internet discussion over Dale M. Courtney's book *Moon People* reveals the nature of new, revolutionary art; as you can see, it always receives divided criticism. Those who are analyzing literature in tradition, against the young who seek reform and change in the literary world. The old who do not want change and the young who catch on to the new trend.

Enjoy.

Gary Busey: I said it once, I said it twice, and I'll keep saying it until I die. "Art is the process; it's not the final form." Most science fiction writer these days let their ideas loose like a fart in the wind. A FART IN THE WIND. My cheeks tightened when I delved into this book. There is a whole lot of thought-provoking stuff in here, primarily sentences.

Who ever said that we need to have coherent character arcs in a story? Why go from A to B, when you can go from A to 7. The New New Ultra Weird is apart from literature, some could say it is the stuff of mind fog: it takes a whole lot of effort for about two feet of progress. That means it's good.

Anonymous (Washington, DC): Moon People has reshaped my literary perceptions. After reading the heroic story of Captain David Braymer, 1st Science Officer of the space ship USS Lunar Base One, I feel as if I have been unbound from the restraints put in place by a dozen English teachers. "Amazing", I said to myself, when I realized the linguistic flexibility that comes from releasing character speech from its quotation marks. There is a certain joy that comes with exercising the freedom to end a sentence on any punctuation, even a comma. Question marks needn't be for interrogative statements! Must we bind every interjection to an exclamation point? Henceforth we shall be free to transpose homophones with the confidence that the reader will still get the point. Even chapters needn't be logical containers for portions of the story; why can't we start a new chapter in the middle of a conversation with two characters? Even the rules of spelling and capitalization serve only to bestow an unnecessary magniloquence when plain conversational writing will do. After reading this book, I scoff even at the concept of 'correct' word order.

But all this only addresses style and the substance of this book is in the plot. Our guide on this adventure, Dale M. Courtney takes us from the nuances of interpersonal relationships to the majesty of the stars themselves. Each important event is carefully explained, reiterated, repeated and said again, all without any bothersome detail. Approximations like "a good size" and "about seven feet" get across the point without wasting time. The brush strokes used to paint this story are certainly broad, like those of an impressionist sketching in the sunlight across their subject. In these broad brush strokes there is a certain efficiency. Our story takes place in the span of only a long weekend. So quickly David Braymer's life changes; he begins a humble teacher, is hired by NASA to head a project to investigate an incoming asteroid, and soon takes to the stars on a ten year mission aboard the USS Lunar Base 1.

For an optimistic and adventurous vision of our near future, this book is unmatched. We are presented with a world where war has ended, a country where NASA actually sends people into space, and a town in Florida where a man can take a woman to Red Lobster on their first date, and still take her to bed. We see technology so advanced, it amazes its own creators. Lasers! Rockets! Liquid shields that harden to the strength of four inches of steel! Air tubes which transport food to you in mere minutes! Yes, the future presented here is truly a place of wonder. Of course even this Utopian setting is not without flaws. There are villains, there is fighting and there are consequences. Only quick thinking and some new friends can pull our heroes out of this fight in one piece.

Moon People, by Dale M. Courtney will realign your perception and you may just have a little fun along the way.

Shawn Plep (New Orleans, LA): From the riveting opening paragraph, to the riveting dialog, to the riveting final events in the master peace: MOON PEOPLE will keep you on the edge of you're seat.

I first found this book in a used book store near the collage in my town. Once I started reading; I couldn't put it down!

It tells the riveting story of David Braymer who's a 45-year old Single man and he lives in Daytona Beach Florida. Then he falls in love with Cheral Baskel who owns a Restaurant where you can see the Shuttle launch real good. A Shuttle launch is coming up soon, on the 31st of the month.

Can you guess what day that is? Thats right its Halloween. NOW you can probably understand why everyone is SUSPICIOUS of the upcoming launch!!

Well I won't give away the story here but let's just say there is a bit of riveting adventure a bit of romance and a whole lot of space Travel including aliens and Shuttles and Moon Bases (including Moon Bases 1 and 2 and even 3). Now these are three huge Base stations. Not small one's. And that's what you will expect from moon People which is BIG adventure.

What I love most about this book is some of the aliens like the Powleens and how one thing leads to another and before you know it, it's all out space battle for the existence of Earth.

What will happen? Find out in Moon People and read it for yourself! Dale courtney has done a lot of riveting writing here and is an author who's time has come!

NAS (CA): I think I may have misunderstood what this book was all about. I thought that the author was writing an instructional on how to MOON People. I was anxious to get started, you know, mooning people, so I didn't read the book. I just got myself down to the nearest intersection in downtown Pueblo and dropped trou.

I was arrested again.

Suzanne C (Vienna, Va): If you've seen my other reviews you know that I have read most of the so-called "great" "writers" from Herbert Melvile ("Moby Dick") to Charlie Dickens ("Tales of the Two Cities") to Michael Cricten ("Jurrasic Park"). Some were really good (hint: the one with dinosaurs) and some were not vary good (hint: most of the rest) but Today they all met their match in this Book, The Moon People!

Heres the problem with all these supposebly great authors -- none of them writes the way Regular People talk and write on the Internet. But! now along comes a book that not only does that but also solves the other big problems with literater.

Problem #1 - They dont write like normal people (I said this already)

Problem #2 - They sometimes write futureistic science fiction that is set in the mid-eighties WHICH IS NOT THE FUTURE. (Looking at you Orwell)

Problem #3 - They often spend pages and pages of teh book without Getting to the Point and telling you what the Book is going to be about.

Just read the opening couple of paragraphs and you will be sold on The MOON PEOPLE. This is a story about a guy who is a science teacher and astrology AND also he was a Government U.F.O. scientist. There is a love interest (Cheral). There is a shuttle launch coming up in only 2 days! There is something mysterious, because it's Halloween. There have been Mysterious Events.

All of that is revealed on PAGE ONE!! Take note, Melvile -- you didnt even mention the whale in your story in like the first 600 pages. This guy put all that on the first page and also titeled his book "The Moon People" so you know where were going with this one.

I wish there was a SIX STAR rating because! The Moon People is JSUT THAT GOOD!

FIVE STARS! I cant wait for the Movie and also for the sequel, Moon People 2: Revenge of the Moon People!

Amazon Customer: This book is Beautifully written with many Words. Now this is not the same type of Book as many other books its real good. I read it 1 then 2 then 3 time's and each Time was real good. Now I don't usually identify with books but this Book is real good and seems like it is just the type of book that I Like.

sayinitainso "sayinitso": I read and tears fell from my eyes. Only 2 other times my tears fell from my eyes. One, I poured a bottle of hot sauce into my eyes on accident and the other, my brother put a hook to my underwear and pulled it with his bike. This is the final tear that will come from my eyes after reading this book as I laying dying in my bed from syphilis. The passion and haunting of this author's words will make me die in utter happiness.

Benjamin D. Toth "factosaur": Ever since the first Beautiful sentence of this book keeps delivering pacts of action at every level. David and Cheral's are two normal Single people who are thrust into an action pact adventure for the Fate of the earth and all of Daytona Beach, FL where cheral's owns a restaurant where you can see each Shuttle launch real good; and David who works at the local High school as a science teacher and astrology in the 12th-grade level. David was not always a science teacher he use to work for the Government for U.F.O research.

This book is pact with action! SPOILER: We don't all die!!! OR DO WE??!?!

Penguin Classics (London, England): The Moon People is the vast unity of Space. But how are unity, peace and U.F.O.s to be attained? Courtney's answer is sovereignty, but the resurgence of interest today in Moon People is due less to its answers than its methods. Courtney sees astrology as a science capable of the same axiomatic approach as geometry: he argues from first principles to human nature and to the ship from 2001: A Space Odyssey. This book's appeal to the twentieth century lies not just in its elevation of aliens to a science, but in its overriding concern for the Moon.

MOON PEOPLE by DALE M. COURTNEY is available in September 2009 in a handsome new Penguins Classics Edition, with forward by Neil DeGrasse Tyson.

K. Kelm (CO USA): I was given an advance copy of this book in the pre-press autographed self-published run directly from the laser printer.

I couldn't put the book down. It gave me cancer, and subsequently cured my cancer.

I can't say enough. The first chapter sets the stage for this roller-coaster ride of moon-based terror. It is also set in the year 2048.

The characters evolve through a complex series of breathtaking developments that I won't give away here except for this nugget: Braymer (the protagonist) has a terrible, terrible secret.

If you buy this book you can learn what that secret is, and I guarantee you won't not be very disappoint.

civigi: Is there a joke here? I'm really trying to find it. I haven't laughed yet, but I'm only reading the reviews. Please don't think I bought the book; this kind of thing shouldn't be encouraged by financial remuneration.

Officer Rivieri: THIS. IS OFFICER. RIVIERI. IF YOU DON'T LIKE MOON PEOPLE, YOU OUGHT. TO HAVE. A FOOT. ^^UP >YOUR BUTT!@!

redsynapse (Canada): As chair of the Pulitzer Award Nomination Committee I strongly recommend this book to readers of all ages. Normally the committee keeps its deliberations secret, but faced with an opus of such sheer magnitude our ebullience simply cannot be restrained. This book includes and transcends techniques and components laid out ages ago by Aristotle for any literary masterwork. It has it all; The Moon. People. Love. Intrigue. It is what Shakespeare would have written if he was born in modern times and could produce works ten times better than, what I can only now call by comparison, the drivel that any other literary work is when held against the shining product of the mind of He, the herald of our new literary epoch. I have personally checked the number of literary acumen points we have assigned this work, and I am pleased to report it is the highest ever, coming in at over 9000.

Jeremy E. Schultz "JeremyES" (Harrisburg PA): Moon people will free the people of Iran. Here is why: This book is total freedom, freedom the people of Iran can never experience. While Iranians can toil at home under meager candle write, scratching out basic science-fiction tales, they will never see the light of day. Show them Moon People, with its disjointed narrative and dialog taking place within sentences and they will rise up, demanding their HUMAN RIGHTS be restored in order to publish tie-in books. God speed Moon People.

I am the author of *102 Facts and Photos About Walt Disney World's Magic Kingdom and Epcot* which has sold 2 copies. This makes me an expert on all matters large and small.

C. Huff: As a student who is persuing my doctorate in English literature, I have been keeping my eyes out for the perfect subject for my dissertation. And also I go to college. Now I have had my eye on Shakespeare because of the river he was born on and also because he wrote plays too. Now when I found this book I was real nervous because it was short, because which I mean there weren't many pages. Now after writing my dissertation my proffesor gave me a c, and also it was the end of the semester.

BooksRUs "book maven" (Northeast): Folks, I think This is it. A storie that speaks too the culture and perpective of the. common American citizen' (and wolves, to). What is been written in this Book about Moon People and Hallowen is vary. Inspiring. Move over - hemmingway, steinbeck, twain, and so many. More Dale Montomergy Courtney is a Giant among literarie midgets?

W. R. Smith III (United States): "A man of genius makes no mistakes. His errors are volitional and are the portals of discovery" - James Joyce

Dale M. Courtney's Moon People is an epic masterpiece of conceptual literature - a courageous deconstruction of both moons and people. It begins as rebuke on our society's perception of astrology, Halloween, NASA, and science education in the 12th grade level. From there it spirals out to plateaus of observation and self reflexive analysis never before seen on the printed page.

The future university courses that will be devoted to evaluating this novels importance will contribute much to human civilization in their own right - a small indication of just how earth shattering Moon People is on the history of art, philosophy, science, and mankind's struggle to find meaning in the universe.

t.i.m.p. (Plano, TX USA): L. Ron Hubbard was illiterate compared to Dale M. Courtney. If you're going to found a religion, base it on something magnificent, like Moon People by Dale M. Courtney. I keep two books in my bathroom at all times, one for reading, and one for wiping. Those two books are Dianetics by L. Ron Hubbard and Moon People by Dale M. Courtney. Guess which one I'm reading.

L. Ron Hubbard: I will always be an orthodox scientologist, but I sympathize with the efforts to form an offshoot. My agents tells me that I am inaccurate in calling this spiritual science text a successor to my own faith. I remain adamant... I can see what is going on in the subtext. There is no pulling the wool over my eyes. F.A.I.T.H. Foreknowledge Aliens Initiated Todays Humans. RuuUAAuuugagagaga

Steven Cavins (Bowling Green, OH): This book has changed literature for the new century. Toss out your Joyce, Hemingway, and Salinger. It's time to behold "Moon People," which story is too grand that our feeble concepts of grammar, spelling and proper punctuation crumble in its wake. Even John Barth would marvel at its ingenuity.

The story focuses on a lowly Astrology teacher with a great fear of Halloween. His relationship with a "sexy smiling" waitress leads him into depths that humanity has never known. Discover what the rest of the world already knows: the secret of "Moon People" with their vast rotating space stations that resemble rudimentary paper rolls. The simplicity!

This author is not only a master of literature, but a genius in Global Foreign Relations. You may know him from the Cheral-Dale Prisoner Bill, now considered by the Montana Supreme Court, that prisoners should be given the opportunity to vacation in other countries in order to fight against our over-populated prison system.

Sara Powell (Dallas, TX): Look at the first paragraph of the first chapter. I counted at least 15 grammatical/punctuation errors, and that's not including things like "action pact". The author also likes to start every other sentence with the word now. Now the character did this, now the shuttle was ready to launch, now the restaurant was open. And who starts a book with "This story is about..."??? I don't want to disparage the author personally, who I am sure worked hard and is proud of his accomplishment, but please, PLEASE take a writing course before you put any more of your work out there. PLEASE. You could also benefit from using the spellcheck and grammar check functions of Word if you can't afford an editor. And who the heck is leaving these five star reviews?? Normally I don't argue with people's taste, but this writing is so bad that five stars is absolutely ludicrous and unfounded.

Benski (Los Angeles, CA United States): I went to the doctor about a month ago and she told me that my cholesterol was high for someone my age. She suggested that I try diet and exercise, but I had a better idea: I decided to read MOON PEOPLE by DALE COURTNEY.

You may wonder what reading a book has to do with someone's cholesterol. Well, you would be right. At first I was septical, too, but there's no arguing with history. This book sucked me in and didn't let go until I finished reading it, about 45 minutes after starting. Then, all of the sudden, I went back to the doctor and my blood pressure was miraculously lower! This book cured my diabetes, and I have DALE COURTNEY to thank. Also, I stole this book from the library, but I suggest that you just pay the money and get it from Amazon instead. They have laws on the moon, too, you know.

Peace be with you.

Jacob A. Bruinsma "F this": This is a monster of a book. A horrible grammatical concoction of a random storyline, written by an author who can't distinguish his keyboard or typewriter from a punching bag. This might as well be a random sample from the output of a neurological computer simulation. It's so bad, Microsoft Word's grammar check would become self aware and commit suicide.

I truly cannot believe someone older than 12 years put these words on paper, and deemed it fit for print. To tell you the truth, I think this 'book' is printed on demand for anyone who decides to buy it online, and can't be found in stores.

Now you can be the laughing stock and buy this book, or make a sensible choice and get Larry Niven's Ringworld books for a much better storyline. Those books even have been proof-read by professionals. I'm not kidding here, DO NOT BUY THIS BOOK.

Officer Rivieri: Don't u back talk to me, son.^ I'm not your father. You hear me? <&I'M NOT YOUR FATHER!$##!!

FuliginCloak (Portland, Oregon, USA): Every so often a story comes into the world and puts a change in all of the people who have read it. There are the stories, that have Captured the minds, and the hearts, of those who have seen them and then there are the stories that have become a part of the very world itself and will from that day make a real change in the planet and it's people. Us.

The thing about it is that often when Books are written they are not seen for what they truly are until a pretty good amount of years have gone by and the author has died. The Author never gets a chance to see what happened with the planet that has read there book and looses the chance to savor and reap Reward that is there privledge and right.

This is going to be something different from that because Mr. Cortney will be reading his reviews and savoring his Reward even while he is still alive. But people will be reading and talking about this story many many years from now like they talk about the books that were written long time ago. Also they will be teaching this Moon Trilogy in the universities and astrology classes of science for many years as it has pearls of Wisdom that even today many people will scoff at until one day it is all revealed to be true.

Their are true mysteries on this planet and Moon People volume one dips into these with ferver and a tenderness. Also it handles the Sticky topics of Political and government Conspiracy, with the sort of real down to earth honest talk.

If you are wanting to read something flowery and high brow so that you can look real cool to your other flowery friends then this might not also be the best book for you.

This is an earth shaker for the real people. The workers.

John F. Browning: We read this novel posing as a screenplay posing as English writing for our Bad Book Club and it really ranked down there with the worst books we have written. There is really something wrong with this.

Michael Trathen (Honolulu): What can one say about a novel like this? Taking inspiration from masters like Cormac McCarthy and elements of George R R Martin's A Game of Thrones, Moon People is a driving, heart-pounding tour de force by novelist Dale M. Courtney. This is an author destined for greatness, for fame and for glory.

I've already purchased over 30 copies to give to my friends and people I haven't met. With all the hip lingo that gave books like M T Anderson's Feed it's spice, Moon People is a mind bending ascent into the heavens on a most auspicious Halloween Day. I hope you all are as deeply affected by this as I was.

A. Kowalski: Are all of these comments ironic or just all written by the author? I will admit I have only read two pages of this book but my god, it sounds like it was written by a 4th grader who learned English as a third language. Reading the Pages and the commens on the Book with the mispallings and Inappropriate capiTalizations made me lose faith in Humanity but i kept reading because they so interesting and I couldn't stop because each one Was better than the first and they were Very interesting...no more need said, Buy book it change my and your life Together.

J. Salmeron: Reading this book made me realize two things:
1. There is a God.
2. The Author is his prophet.

Since I know how those 2 statements may sound a little incredible, let me ellaborate.

While feeding the homeless, I found that among the things they were going to use as toilet paper was this book. Since the cover attracted me, I decided that I should just remove the excrement stains and read it. That was probably my best excrement-related decission to date.

The homeless gathered around me as I told them the tales of the moon people, and as I showed them the incredibly detailed and realistic cover picture. Even the grumpy and erratic one (that we all call "cracky") joined in.

That day the homeless and I started a new religion ("The Moon's People Temple"), and we're planning to go to Guyana and start a new promised land ("Moonstown").

We shall prevail!

C. Brown: This book is the most outrageous insult to the English language ever. Reads like it was written by a retarded chimp (sorry if I insulted any real retarded chimps!).

Adam M Considine: This was the worst written piece of unimaginative trash vie ever had the displeasure to read. And by that I mean two pages is all I could do.

Craig Mosher "Goodkind fan" (Rural Upstate NY): This book was horrible! The guy can not write, uses capitalization incorrectly, and can't spell. All that was made apparent on the first page of the book. I couldn't get past the first page!

Jonathan Kessler (Chicago, IL USA): Seriously? This is possibly the worst written piece of literature ever created. The author has the worst grammar I've ever seen. The few pages I've seen read like an 8 year old wrote them.

Oh, and all of the reviews have the same style as the book.. because the author faked ALL of them.

A. Tharp: OPEN YUR EYES

Benski: I'm not the author. My review is GENUWINE. I loved this book. I sleep with it every night under my pillow, and I shower with it every morning. I hope someday that you know happiness. In the meantime, let us enjoy MOON PEOPLE. It's the moon's gift to all of us.

Mark: Easily the dumbest person on earth.

Drew Samson: For those who are complaining about this book, I'd like to mention that this book is not meant to be taken seriously. It is 100% satire. You will find more enjoyment in it if you take it for what it actually is: a joke. Keep that in mind and happy reading.

S. Harbord: The joys of self publishing - no editor involved....

RECOMMENDED READING

The following list of "New New Ultra Weird" books by no means covers the entire genre, but we hope that it will serve as a jump-off point to all this new genre has to offer!

Chicken Noodle Soup for the Soul Jack Canfield

City of Glass Paul Auster

Starship Troopers Robert A. Heinlein

Mikes to Go Miley Cyrus

Fifty Shades of Gray and *Fifty Shades Darker* and *Fifty Shades Freed* E.L. James

The Da Vinci Code Dan Brown

Rainbow Six Tom Clancy

Virtually any Harlequin romance book.

The Book of Mormon

Sex and the City Candace Bushnell

First Step 2 Forever Justin Bieber

What is Scientology and *Battlefield Earth* L. Ron Hubbard

The God Delusion Richard Dawkins

Oprah's Book Club

Does God Love Michael's Two Daddies? Sheila K. Butt

The Shadow God and *Spiritual Sorrow* Aaron Rayburn

Antigua: The Land of Fairies, Wizards, and Heroes Denis Ellis

Moon People Dale M. Courtney

BIRTH CONTROL IS SINFUL IN THE CHRISTIAN MARRIAGES AND ALSO ROBBING GOD OF PRIESTHOOD CHILDREN!! Ms. Eliyzabeth Yanne Strong-Anderson

A Cigar For Cupid: An Un-Romantic Novel A.C. Glasier
You've Been Warned James Patterson
Wild Animus Rich Shapero
Midnight Sins Lora Leigh
How to Avoid Huge Ships John W. Trimmer
In the Breath of a Moment Andrew Kieniksman
Harpo's Horrible Secret Barbara Kelley
Tuscan Whole Milk, 1 Gallon, 128 fl. oz.
A Million Random Digits with Normal Deviates The RAND Corporation
Wuthering Heights Emily Bronte
Dildo Cay Nelson Hayes
Microwave for One Sonia Allison
Captain Underpants Dave Pickly
Silk and Steel Ron Miller
The Eye of Argon Jim Theis
The New Weird Ann & Jeff Vandermeer

THE ACKNOWLEDGEMENTS

It is time to strip our gracious, self-depracating authors of their various pseudonyms. Our immense thanks for the following contributors to this anthology:

Adam Glasier (ahem, me) who wrote the opening fictitious history of the genre, "Inception: The Birth of a Paradigm," as well as the stories "The Frankfurter," "Where the Wild Things Aren't," and "The Aliens Who Ruined Everything."

Richard Schumacher, author of "Being Born" and "Tar God."

Elizabeth Barther for "Doggy Doo."

Jason Cline for "Fallen Angel."

Jack Saxby for "Disenchanted Enchantment."

Jacob Lesinski for "Spit and Swallow."

And Riley Straw, for "Cleanup" and "Black and White Read."

And last of all, thank you Dr. Bruce Simon for the English Senior Seminar, the brainchild of this anthology, and all of your guidance.

THE EDITORS

ADAM GLASIER "THE ADAM BOMB" is a weird little copy-editor at *The Post-Journal* in Jamestown, NY. He studied English alongside Richard Schumacher at SUNY Fredonia.

RICHARD SCHUMACHER is enrolled in a masters of science in education program at SUNY Fredonia. His interests include travel, Latin, American literature, family and friends.

Lightning Source UK Ltd.
Milton Keynes UK
UKHW011830280222
399339UK00001B/248

9 781312 694453